TAROT FOR CHANGE

TAROT
FOR
CHANGE

USING THE CARDS FOR
SELF-CARE, ACCEPTANCE
AND GROWTH

Jessica Dore

Illustrations by Xaviera López

HAY
HOUSE

HAY HOUSE

Carlsbad, California • New York City
London • Sydney • New Delhi

Published and distributed in the United States of America by:
Penguin Life, an imprint of Penguin Random House LLC, 1745 Broadway,
New York, NY 10019

Published in the United Kingdom by:
Hay House UK Ltd, The Sixth Floor, Watson House,
54 Baker Street, London W1U 7BU
Tel: +44 (0)20 3927 7290; Fax: +44 (0)20 3927 7291; www.hayhouse.co.uk

Published in Australia by:
Hay House Australia Ltd, 18/36 Ralph St, Alexandria NSW 2015
Tel: (61) 2 9669 4299; Fax: (61) 2 9669 4144; www.hayhouse.com.au

Published in India by:
Hay House Publishers India, Muskaan Complex, Plot No.3, B-2,
Vasant Kunj, New Delhi 110 070
Tel: (91) 11 4176 1620; Fax: (91) 11 4176 1630; www.hayhouse.co.in

Text © Jessica Dore, 2021

Illustrations: Xaviera López
Book design: Daniel Lagin

A catalogue record for this book is available from the British Library.

Tradepaper ISBN: 978-1-78817-710-8
E-book ISBN: 978-1-78817-712-2
Audiobook ISBN: 978-1-78817-711-5

Printed and bound in Great Britain by TJ Books Limited, Padstow, Cornwall.

MIX
Paper from
responsible sources
FSC
www.fsc.org   FSC® C013056

For my parents

Contents

SECTION I

SECTION II

The Minor Arcana

SECTION III

TAROT FOR CHANGE

SECTION I

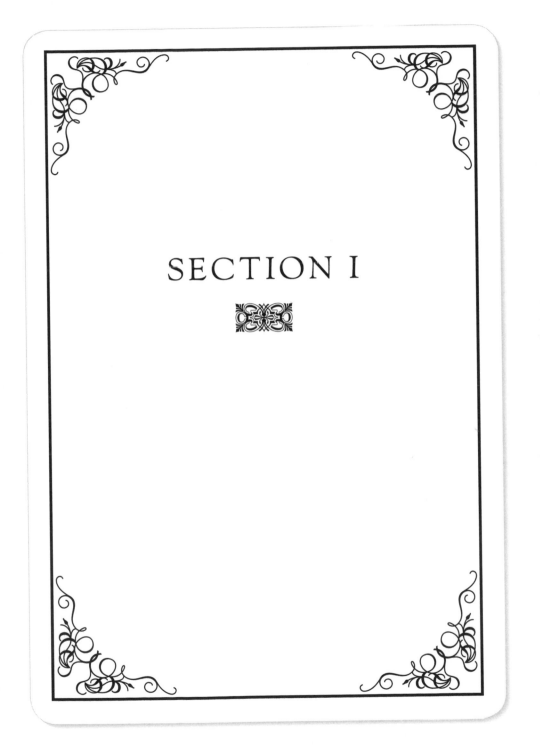

What Is Tarot?

arot is a book of seventy-eight secrets that reveal themselves over time. The cards have meanings, but they often shape-shift, so depending on the context, a card might appear in the form of an aid, charm, talisman, or benediction. Though the set of cards as we know them today are believed to have first appeared in fifteenth-century Europe during the Renaissance, the secrets and totems tucked inside are said to have their origins in ancient Egypt and Greece.

Legend has it that the mystics of Egypt hid their secrets for spiritual evolution—about how to attain the ideal of union with the Absolute—inside a set of playing cards. Tucking secrets into card form was a way for them to ensure the preservation of hard-won wisdom through human vice. They trusted more in the drive to gamble and play than they did the human desire to read sacred texts, or learn through oral transmission, and knew that some would "play" tarot without ever using the cards to ascend. But for those inclined toward spiritual growth, the cards would function like seventy-eight magic portals, with secrets inside.

This is legend, which means it is unhistorical and unverifiable. There's no physical proof to support it. But tarot, as you'll see if you have not already, provides a path toward reclaiming the imagination from the grips of doubt and rationalism. Toward reawakening the part in us with the audacity to know without material evidence.

These days, people use cards for all kinds of reasons. Pulling cards is a way to summon synchronicity, a sacred process by which we experience the invisible connections between the inner and outer worlds.

It is also a practice that activates potential, planting the early radicles of possibility in the soil of the heart so that the roots can grow sturdy. Strong enough to sustain the slow growth of a fruit or a flower.

When necessary, a spread of tarot cards can be like a tapestry onto which we project our inner life safely and without harming ourselves or others. Because projection is a natural and healthy function of the human imagination, this is one way to harness its power and use it for good. The externalization of internal experience onto a physical ob-ject like a card creates some distance that gives us room to breathe, shifts how we relate to ourselves, and offers a new vantage point to look from. The cards allow us to safely see and understand the less palatable aspects of ourselves.

A tarot reading, whether done for oneself or others, can be a ritual in times of initiation into an important life stage or chapter. The cards have a maieutic, or midwifing, function, in which they ask questions as part of a birthing process that brings forth new life. Questions that broaden rather than narrow down. Sometimes new life is trying to come out backward or upside down and needs a bit of coaxing to turn. Tarot is a tool for finding the right spots to press down on to get things moving safely.

Sometimes, after cards have been pulled, you might leave with a narrative that's expansive and life giving. With visions of first tulip tips in newly thawed earth or pink buds on a branch. Other times, a story needs to be stripped down to what's essential, and then you might walk with the scent of dry rotting leaves or the sound of a raven caw echoing between your ears. Either way, you can expect to leave with more ques-tions than you came with. This is good. Questions are passageways to new life.

It is not the job of a card reader to promise revelations, because that's not how secrets work. The seventy-eight arcana, the mysteries great and small, are to be approached with the respect due to elders, as entities unto themselves whose trust must be earned. As is the case with any companion, where there is curiosity, commitment, respect, and a genuine wish to understand, the cards will tell you secrets over time. You can be sure of that.

Tarot and Psychology:
A Brief History

arot is often considered more a spiritual practice than a psychological one, but it is inherently psychological, and psychology is inherently spiritual. In fact, the word *psychology* comes from the word *psyche*, which means "soul" or "breath" in Greek. Though the psychology field has changed over years of theory and practice, to a certain extent it will always be an art of coming to know the soul.

Sigmund Freud, who is regarded in the West as the father of modern psychology, sought to understand the human psyche through the process of psychoanalysis. A goal of psychoanalytic work was to make the unconscious conscious. When you think about the trope of a person lying on a couch next to an analyst in a suit with a clipboard saying, "Tell me about your father," they're doing psychoanalysis. That therapeutic process would often involve a deep dive into early childhood experiences in order to better understand one's experiences in the present day.

Carl Jung, who was a student of Freud's, developed theories of a collective unconscious—a sort of psychic undercurrent that he believed all humans share and that might account for common drives, motivations, and behaviors that transcend the bounds of cultural and geographic difference. The collective unconscious has been described as a sort of shared psychological inheritance that reveals itself through dreams, myths, and fairy tales, and in social dynamics of power and oppression. Unlike the personal unconscious, which contains the dimensions of our individual experience that have been driven underground often through environmental and social conditioning, the collective unconscious is believed by some to be the home of archetypes.

Jung thought of archetypes as universal symbols and images with meanings that all humans share. I'm not sure I agree that archetypes have the same universal meanings to all humans, but I can see how some resonate across cultures. For each of us, the archetype of mother can activate something—though not the same thing for all of us—as does the archetypal theme of death. And I agree with Jungian analyst Marie-Louise von Franz's assertion that when an archetypal image shows up—as might happen in a tarot card reading, for example—the person witnessing that image "will become aware of new, previously unrecognized possibilities and through them will experience a fresh influx of energy; for the archetypes possess a numinous quality and function as a hidden source of energy." We aren't all going to experience archetypes or symbols in the same way, nor should we be expected to. But they can stir something in us and tell us something, if we allow space for that.

Jung believed that the collective unconscious influenced our individual lives and held keys to meaning making, psychological development, and individuation (a process through which a person achieves a sense of individual identity separate from the collective). Through psychoanalysis, a person might learn to move flexibly between the explicit content of the conscious mind and the tacit symbolic material of the unconscious. In archetypal terms, we might say the hope was that a person could begin to exist somewhere in the tension between the village and the forest, civilization and the wild, to be both emperor and empress in the right place and time.

Jung also contributed ideas about the therapeutic value of synchronicity, which he defined as "a meaningful coincidence" of external and internal events that are not connected by any discernible cause and effect relationship. An example of synchronicity is when you suddenly think of a friend you haven't seen in years, only to receive a call from that person soon after. Such a thing could be bare coincidence, but to the person inclined toward meaning making, it can also hint at a connection between the external and internal, dimensions that generally appear as separate and distinct from one another.

When an internal event, such as a thought of an old friend, "syncs up" with an external event, like that old friend calling, we might begin to sense a link between what we experience as an individual and what we understand as a whole. Synchronicity is, in the words of ecologist Robin Wall Kimmerer, "a reminder of elegant connections." Exploring relationships between things that cannot be explained by simple cause and effect is a doorway to understanding the relationship between psyche, a more collective consciousness, and matter. When synchronicities occur, as is so often the case when we pull tarot cards and they nail the details of our lives with astounding accuracy, it may be that something previously hidden in the unconscious is trying to emerge. And that it might just be bubbling up in order to help us evolve.

Today, Jung might have been seen as more of an artist or philosopher than a scientist. His exploration of mystery through the fields of philosophy, anthropology, myth, religion, and spirituality informed the development of his style of analytical psychology. And he genuinely believed that the symbols found within old stories, astrology, and even the tarot contained keys to understanding the psyche.

Jung's understanding of archetype and individuation is useful here because it brings the power and appeal of tarot into clearer focus. Many of us find that once we start working with tarot, we get hooked. And my sense is that this is because its symbolic language instantly and powerfully connects us with a collective consciousness of some kind—whether that be universal or cultural. Pulling cards places us back in space and time as part of something greater than ourselves and reminds us that whatever we're experiencing, we are not alone. In a time marked by growing isolation, separation, and loneliness, that in itself holds the promise of a deep medicine.

Around the turn of the twentieth century, the field of psychology began to make a shift from something that more closely resembled a humanities discipline to something that looked more like a science. Unlike analytical psychology, with its emphasis on memories and internal life, behaviorism approached psychology through the study of what could be observed; not only what was happening for someone internally but also what they could be physically seen doing. Ivan Pavlov's notorious concept of classical conditioning showed the ways that behavior can be learned, and B. F. Skinner looked at how future behavior is shaped and influenced by the outcomes of past and present behavior. This emphasis on objective and experimental studies can be credited with shifting the psychology field from something perhaps more creative and philosophical to a scientific discipline.

Information gathered from the study of behavior eventually led to the development of cognitive behavioral therapy (CBT) by psychologist Aaron Beck. CBT combines an emphasis on the internal and external by focusing on the interaction between thoughts, feelings, and behavior in order to help people make changes in support of sustained well-being.

Today, behavioral therapies are widely used in the counseling field. This is partly because they are evidence based, meaning that they are built on what science has shown works—at least in certain circumstances—to support behavior change. Because of the emphasis on behavior, which is more observable than internal or invisible experiences in the realms of thoughts, feelings, and energy, the outcomes of behavioral interventions like CBT are more measurable. This means they're easier to research and can inform a standard of care. Clinicians want to use what's been shown to work, and while behavioral therapy's emphasis on cause and effect allows us to isolate targets for treatment that often yield powerful outcomes, the old ideas about synchronicity, collective consciousness, and the quest for life meaning that goes beyond individual values often fall to the wayside in this model of care. Efforts to boil the study of the soul down to a science have led to great strides in the treatment of mental illness but have relegated mystery and magic to the edges.

One of the foundational secrets of tarot is that many things can be true at once. The scientific study of behavior is not at odds with explorations of a collective consciousness, the therapeutic use of symbol and archetype, or the application of mythology and folktales for healing. And while the framework of evidence-based practice is built on the assumption that the only legitimate evidence is that which has been gathered through the scientific method, I'd argue that when something stands the test of time, as the symbols embedded in the tarot have, that's proof of a certain degree of efficacy as well.

We don't have to dig far into evidence-based therapy models to find that a lot of them aren't at odds with mystic philosophies at all and in many cases are even deeply compatible. This is a testament to the fact that, just as Jung believed the collective unconscious affected all people, so do the cosmologies and belief systems of our ancestors. The scientific method is, at the end of the day, a human-centered operation. That means that research questions, models, and instruments for measurement can never achieve full objectivity or exemption from the influence of those who came before. Old beliefs and assumptions about the nature of things are so embedded in our cultural institutions that, like fish in water, we don't see them unless we really look. Once we do, we begin to see that they permeate our experience from every possible direction.

Before we had science as we know it today, we had other ways of knowing. And those ways inform, at least to some extent, the way that today's scientists think, feel, and do their work. And while science is a beautiful and fascinating way of studying and gathering information, it is one way. It is a valuable way, but it is not the only way. Through our discussion of the tarot's major arcana, we'll touch more on the trappings of binaries—like science and spirituality, new and old—and the quest toward a way of being that transcends such false divisions. Where we wouldn't have to pick sides but could be with, revere, and accommodate all that is, simultaneously.

When it comes to bridging the perceived rift between science and spirituality, an emerging and appropriately named "third wave" of behavioral therapies seems to be a move in a positive direction. Therapies like mindfulness-based cognitive therapy, dialectical behavior therapy (DBT), and acceptance and commitment therapy (ACT) blend wisdom from mystic traditions like Buddhism and yoga—including mindfulness, acceptance, and compassion—with behavioral science data to develop powerful interventions. After the pendulum swing from a more creative and philosophical approach to understanding the human soul, toward a more objective and scientific one, it's wonderful to see the field catch a balance someplace in the middle, synthesizing technologies from both the scientific and the spiritual. As it is said in the philosophical laws of the Western mystery tradition of Hermeticism, rhythm compensates.

My Story

I came to the psychology field by way of book publishing. After college I moved to California, where I was hired to be a publicist for a self-help and psychology book publisher. My job there was to publicize clinical psychology manuals for therapists and self-help workbooks that used evidence-based interventions to help readers with things like depression, anxiety, OCD, and eating disorders.

As an uninitiated layperson, I felt like I was getting an insider's glimpse into something that felt esoteric, though I didn't know that word then. The books I worked on contained skills, techniques, and insights that were marketed specifically to a select group of people—therapists—who would then share them with clients in the time and manner in which they saw fit. These were secrets, really, in that to an extent they were kept under "lock and key," tucked into pricey books with titles that started with phrases like *The Clinician's Guide to...* and that sort of thing.

Though anyone with the financial means could technically buy these types of books, most wouldn't. It was set up that way. Somehow I, a poet with a communications degree who had not undergone the initiations one typically would to get access to these secrets—graduate school, internships, clinical training—was getting access to them. What luck. And it wasn't long before I realized that the secrets I was reading about were incredibly potent.

I started to apply what I was learning about things like emotion regulation, distress tolerance, cognitive reframing, behavioral activation, radical acceptance, mindfulness, and self-compassion to my own life, and experienced firsthand the transformative power they could have. I'd never heard of these things before, and I wondered why that was. I wondered why, if they were so effective, they weren't more widely available, why I hadn't learned about them in school or from my parents. I wondered whether that could change.

In the early days at the publishing company, I became interested in tarot. I started studying Pamela Colman Smith's illustrations, which are popularly referred to as the Rider-Waite tarot deck (though in this book I'll refer to it as the Rider-Waite-Smith deck, to acknowledge Colman Smith's invaluable contributions). Here was another set of secrets, which at that time were also pretty guarded in that they weren't understood in the mainstream as something containing value for everyday people. To my surprise and delight, they contained a lot of similar wisdoms as the books I was reading for work.

I didn't know this at the time but the Rider-Waite-Smith deck is underpinned by the philosophy of Hermeticism, a Western mystery tradition. An ideal of Hermeticism is to experience the *totality* of things, to understand that things which may appear to be in opposition to one another—internal and external, above and below, good and bad—are actually "identical in nature," existing together on a spectrum where they are different only in degree.

This way of understanding the world has a deep compatibility with dialectical behavior therapy (DBT), which aims to cultivate a way of living and thinking that embodies a both/and rather than an either/or mindset. Dialectical thinking involves holding space in our awareness for things that seem to be in conflict but are in fact both real and true. For instance, a DBT therapist will support a client in accepting a kind of dual reality: that the client is both doing their best, and still needs to do better. This is just one example of the many overlaps between the concepts found in tarot and contemporary psychology.

After a few years working with the cards privately and seeing the transformative power of their secrets, I began writing about tarot on the internet, first in a blog that very few people read and then on social media, pairing Colman Smith's illustrations with ideas from different therapies like DBT, cognitive behavioral therapy (CBT), and acceptance and commitment therapy (ACT). I knew how powerful these seemingly disparate sets of ideas and images had been in transforming my own life and wanted to share the secrets I'd been granted access to in a way that others could also hear them.

At that point, I was still a layperson taking "insider" information out of expensive textbooks written for clinicians and sharing it for free on social media. And though I eventually did go back to school for a master's degree in social work, during which time I trained as a therapist in behavioral health clinics, I decided not to pursue the route of clinical training any further after graduation. I liked my role as a go-between, an edge dweller, a walker between worlds.

This offering, *Tarot for Change*, is a book of secrets that I've gathered from my years walking the perimeters of two fields that hold powerful technologies for transformation and growth. Some of what I'll share here are secrets only in that they have, until recently, been hidden away by institutions that would prefer only certain individuals with particular credentials have the power to keep and share them. And while I find the idea of some wisdom remaining sacred through secrecy incredibly romantic, I am thankful to be witnessing an unprecedented level of secret telling by clinicians who see the value in sharing information with the public that was once accessible only in the context of individual or group therapy.

Other secrets contained here are so called because they have more to do with spirituality, an area of life that contains an inherent dimension of mystery, I think, because we have yet to come up with a reliable way to measure or quantify spirit. These are the secrets that the tarot itself has told me through years of engaging with the symbols, noticing where they show up in the books I read, the stories I'm told, the songs I hear, and the dreams I have, and in the rituals, prayers, and ways of my culture and the culture of those who came before me.

I think it's important to share with all readers—not only for the sake of clarity and transparency but also for its mythic and symbolic significance—that while I do hold a degree and license in social work and have indeed undergone the initiation required in order to be seen as legitimate by the field, I am not a therapist and I do not practice psychotherapy. As I said before, I prefer to dwell on the edges, in the liminal space between categories that are so often set in opposition to one another, like laypeople and clinicians, or tarot card readers and licensed therapists. Because to stand on the edge allows us to see from a new vantage point, and therefore gives us a shot at innovating in spaces that might benefit from a different perspective.

I've been listening closely a long time, and one thing I've learned from folktales and myths and the keepers of such stories is that when a society is as troubled as ours is, we're wise to scan the outskirts and tune our awareness to the margins. Because the old stories tell us that that's where the medicine comes from: the margins, not the center. And so in choosing not to be a therapist or a tarot card reader but to exist somewhere between the two, gathering words and pictures that tell secrets and sharing them, this is where I like to think I've set up shop, and where I'll be for now. And this is the space from which I write these words to you.

Getting to Know the Cards

hen I first started writing publicly about tarot and psychology, I mostly worried about what others in the mental health field would think. I was concerned that they'd think tarot had no place in delivering evidence-based insights that could help people understand the relationship between thoughts, feelings, and behavior, or perform any other therapeutic function, for that matter. But I was pleasantly surprised to find that not only do more psychotherapists than I'd imagined use tarot in their work, quite a few were also eager for more resources that could help them bridge the evidence-based therapies and techniques they'd trained in, with the cards.

I have, however, gotten a bit of pushback from tarot purists who assert that the cards have one strict meaning and are not open to interpretations as loose as I sometimes use. In my excitement about the clinical potential of tarot and admitted esoteric naivety, I've been on record a number of times comparing the cards to the Rorschach test— ambiguous ink blots on pieces of paper used in psychiatric evaluations. Unfortunately, this comparison negates the reality that the images on the cards do mean things, things that when understood and applied properly can be used as keys to unlock the mysteries of change and transformation. Now, having deepened my own understanding of and relationship with the cards, I understand why some might struggle with my more exoteric, or practical, interpretations of the cards.

Years ago, when I began a daily Ashtanga yoga practice, I didn't see it as a spiritual thing, necessarily. I knew yoga was an ancient spiritual tradition rooted in India, but as a twenty-four-year-old woman working to overcome years of self-destructive behaviors, I was mostly concerned with learning to take better care of myself, be inside my body, and build strength and flexibility. When I asked my teacher if there were books I should read, he told me—and I'm paraphrasing— that yoga was something to be experienced rather than intellectualized about. I think this is what he'd been taught by his teacher, Sri K. Pattabhi Jois of Mysore in southern India, who had reportedly taught that yoga was 99 percent practice and 1 percent theory. I took the point and showed up to practice, day after day. And over time I started to understand—not at an intellectual level but a felt and energetic one—what this practice of yoga, a word having to do with *union*, was about.

I'm sharing this example of my experience with yoga not because I see it as appropriate for me to talk about what yoga is or is not—I don't. I share it because I think it has some important things in common with a tarot practice. It's true that when worked with in earnest, this set of cards, like a yoga practice, holds profound spiritual data. But as products of an achievement-oriented global culture, we often need entry points that appeal to the practicalities of our daily lives and offer a "promise" that will motivate us to engage. And so if you've come to tarot because you want to build a self-care practice, to better understand your relationships, to navigate a big career or lifestyle change, or to better know your self, let me be the first to welcome you. You do not need to career yourself deep into the teachings of the ancient mystery schools, or even know "what the symbols mean," to glean value from the cards. You simply need to show up. Preferably with a willingness and curiosity. And let your commitment to the cards work its magic.

Experience has revealed to me that using tarot cards even, and perhaps especially when, one has no prior knowledge of their meanings can be an incredibly powerful practice. When not bound by rigid definitions, the cards work almost like a magic elixir that brings latent creative, intuitive, and meaning-making abilities to the fore.

With sustained use, the cards can foster self-trust, introspection, and an interior grounding that can offset the tendency to look only outward for answers.

Just as the anonymous author of *Meditations on the Tarot* wrote that the major arcana are magical entities unto themselves, occultist Aleister Crowley wrote in his *Book of Thoth* that "the cards of the Tarot are living individuals" and that it is always necessary to consider not only the meaning of the cards but also the living, dynamic relationship between the cards and the practitioner. His book, like many that have offered analyses of the cards, strove to offer "the general character of each card" but reminded the reader that they "cannot reach any true appreciation of them without observing their behaviour over a long period" and "can only come to an understanding of the Tarot through experience."

Crowley asserted that it would never be enough for the practitioner to simply intensify their intellectual study of the card meanings "as objective things; he must use them; he must live with them. They, too, must live with him." The ideal way to do this, according to Crowley, was contemplation. Which, contrary to popular belief, is not a solo endeavor but a participatory process (*con* meaning *with*) that includes seeking and seeing what is reflected. To do this we have to expand our gaze beyond the explicit—the stuff we might read in a book of interpretations, perhaps—to include also the peripheral. We have to open ourselves up to receive what wants to shine back.

The cards do have meanings, it's true. But they—like everything else in this world—are not islands and they are not static. Their meanings shape-shift with time and in context, depending to a great extent on the beholder and what that person is ready, willing, and able to receive. The impact that a card has on a person is not about the person's intellectual understanding of the card's significance. Rather, each card is like an old brass bell that, when rung, holds the potential to send a ripple through our being that activates latent pools and pockets of wisdom.

The secrets I'll share here are derived from some combination of "traditional" meanings (via Arthur Waite, Rachel Pollack, Aleister Crowley, Lon Milo DuQuette, and the anonymous author of *Meditations on the Tarot*) and the lenses through which I tend to view the world, including but not limited to behavioral and analytic psychology, mythology and folktales, spiritual practice, and my own personal learning history.

The Architecture of the Seventy-Eight-Card Deck

 seventy-eight-card, four-suit tarot deck contains two main sections: the major arcana and the minor arcana. The word *arcana*, with its roots in the Latin *arcanus*, means "secrets," and seasoned readers will tell you that when you've been in the right relationship with the cards long enough, they start to spill their secrets. By *right relationship* I mean that you don't go around demanding revelations, instead you show up with regularity and reverence. I mean that you come with offerings, of attention and energy, resources more precious than frankincense and myrrh. And that you open yourself up to receiving as well. I mean that you always remember: a secret is something that is given, not something you simply take or that is fabricated to suit your needs.

And so in each deck we have major secrets and minor ones. The greater, major secrets relate to overarching themes on what we might call a path toward re-membering, toward wholeness, or that we might just call a healing journey. The lesser, minor secrets explore the four domains of human being—spiritual, emotional, behavioral, and intellectual—and these are represented by the four suits—wands, cups, pentacles, and swords.

THE MAJOR ARCANA

At the very beginning of social work school I learned about the person-in-environment perspective, which focuses on the influence of context on individual well-being. Later, I learned to toggle skillfully between identifying when to intervene at the individual level and when to intervene at the systemic. In social work, a combination of intervention at the individual level and at the systemic level generally yields the desired change and healing—a nod to the importance of taking context into account—and tarot is similar. The cards can be used to help us understand ourselves as individuals, and they can be used to help us understand ourselves as part of a larger context.

Similarly, there are two ways to approach the major arcana, as individuals or as part of a larger story. New readers sometimes prefer to study the twenty-two major mysteries as stand-alone entities with their own distinct meanings, and there is nothing wrong with this; in fact, most of the reflections in this book will approach the cards this way. But it's illuminating, if and when you feel ready, to consider the major arcana as a whole. The twenty-two-card sequence can be viewed as a story and road map for any questing person. Along the way, its arc reveals a series of steps and lessons that count toward realization of reality, of seeing ourselves as who we truly are and life as it is. And so for all those interested in using tarot as a spiritual road map, come lean in and tune your ear.

In counseling and recovery programs, people are commonly asked to identify their "why" at the outset of treatment—the things that are most precious to them that make doing the hard work worth it. This is one of the reasons why I find it helpful to begin discussions of the major arcana at the culmination of the sequence, the World. The World is the last card in the major arcana. It is the end of the journey, the sought-after, hard-to-attain treasure.

Joseph Campbell has said, "The mystery of life is beyond all human conception. Everything we know is within the terminology of the concepts of being and not being, many and single, true and untrue. We always think in terms of opposites. But God, the ultimate, is beyond the pairs of opposites, that is all there is to it." The World stands for that "ultimate" place, beyond opposites. An experience of totality, where all things no matter how seemingly conflicted can exist together and false separations dissolve, is both the ideal of the mystic and the modern dialectical behavior therapist.

The mythical teacher Hermes Trismegistus instructs aspirants of Hermeticism to "grasp in your thought all of this at once, all times and places, all substances and qualities and magnitudes together. Then you can apprehend God." Similarly, a dialectical behavior therapist encourages the synergy of opposites by supporting a client to do two things that appear to be contradictory: accept themselves fully and work to do better. In psychoanalysis, the World might represent the integration of the conscious and unconscious, of ego and shadow. This integration requires a reclamation of all the parts in ourselves that we were born with but learned to drive underground, the parts we were told—in whatever way—were unacceptable and unwanted. In myths and old stories, the World symbolizes the "happily ever after," a marriage of princes and princesses as symbols of the reuniting of the complementary forces of will and imagination, or reconciliation with a rejected outcast twin who'd been thrown into the forest at birth.

The World tells of a return from interiority to interdependence. Of learning to experience the world as it is, in all its contradiction and difference, where both the village and forest exist side by side and have their time and place. Perhaps the way our minds process the world—as something divided, parceled off, and split up—is a projection of our own internal partitions, things accepted and things exiled. The World is a promise that we might one day be able to access the wholeness of our being and the wholeness to which we belong, in all its wild ambiguity.

The Fool is often understood as an animating energy that moves through the major arcana sequence, rather than a fixed point in the story, like the little silver top hat or shoe that moves across a Monopoly board with each roll of the dice. The Fool's number in the major arcana sequence is zero, shaped like an egg, and signifies pure potential. In tarot, like old stories, gender functions in a symbolic way, with men and women as visual representations of complementary energies whose interplay manifests in different ways. The Fool is a nonbinary character, which stands for an innocence of the limitations of seeing everything always in pairs of opposites. The Fool tells of a potential for human consciousness that exists outside of the divisive thinking that has plagued the human race since time out of mind. Like Adam and Eve in the Garden of Eden before they've eaten the forbidden fruit and learned that they are different from each other.

The Fool's entrance onto the path of the major arcana symbolizes the experience each and every one of us had when we stepped into the field of space and time at birth. Immediately, we enter a land of duality, and so does the Fool find themselves met with a series of opposites.

First, the Fool encounters the Magician and the High Priestess, which represent the conscious and unconscious, ego and shadow, explicit and tacit, respectively. Next, the Empress and the Emperor symbolize nature and civilization, the wild and the domesticated, the free range and the structured. Then, the Hierophant, an intermediary and interpreter of great spiritual mysteries, holds the duality of above and below, spiritual and material. The Lovers holds another image of the above and below paradigm, as well as symbols of masculine and feminine—in some decks this card is called "the choice." And finally, the Chariot depicts a white sphinx and a black sphinx, which again symbolize ego and shadow, light and dark, the conscious and unconscious dimensions of the psyche. Though this card is often read as one about success and achievement, it has little to offer the aim of integration. Though the two sphinxes are seated side by side, they are merely held in balance by a skilled public-facing persona. Not that this isn't an accomplishment, it is. Even a life's work. But beyond that threshold, there's more.

Joseph Campbell said that the dualities in the field of space and time were not the end point but rather "a springboard to spring you into the transcendent... to go past duality." Once beyond the Chariot, the Fool moves from the early mysteries—those having to do with family, society, the organization of human life—and into what I've come to understand as the middle mysteries. Here, they advance beyond the lessons contained inside the limits of space and time toward those that go beyond a this-or-that way. Internal life simply doesn't work like that.

It doesn't take much to recognize that the strategies we use to solve problems in our external lives don't work so well when we apply them to our internal lives. You can't fix grief, you can only learn how to engage it with curiosity and gentleness—as Strength, the first of the middle arcana, teaches. There are new mysteries to explore here, more secrets to learn.

Here, from Strength to Temperance, the Fool encounters mysteries of the internal dimension: force (represented by Strength), peace (represented by the Hermit), change (represented by the Wheel of Fortune), cause and effect (represented by Justice), acceptance (represented by the Hanged Man), transformation (represented by Death), and balance (represented by Temperance). Having moved from force to balance, the Fool encounters the Devil, which symbolizes in part the delicate tension between the material and spiritual, and the inescapable realities of existing as an earthbound being. The Tower brings the revelation that serves to liberate the Fool from interiority, their now lifelong sense of separation from the world to which they know they belong but have felt undeniably exiled from since the day they entered the field of space and time.

The Tower's fall marks the Fool's entrance into what we might call a set of celestial secrets, and here we encounter a set of symbols representing a kind of consciousness that is collective rather than individual: the Star, the Moon, and the Sun, which are perhaps collective counterparts to the Fool, the High Priestess, and the Magician. They are the animating force of growth and evolution (the Star), a collective unconscious (the Moon), and a collective conscious (the Sun). Here in the celestial realm, the Fool has moved beyond understanding themselves as solely separate but also as part of a whole.

Judgment presents an image of resurrection, rebirth, and ascension, where the Fool remembers their place in a broader scheme of humanity and embraces a "calling" or purpose that both relates to the whole and also makes them unique. This balance of the self as both distinct and common ultimately leads the Fool back to the World, into the totality of things.

THE MINOR ARCANA

The minor arcana, or "lesser mysteries," of the tarot offer secrets about how to navigate daily life as a member of the human race with the four capacities humans are born with, represented by the four suits. The four capacities or domains of experience are: energy, emotions, behavior, and intellect. These are connected with each of the four suits: wands, cups, pentacles, and swords, respectively. Each suit gives information about the domain itself—the energetic, emotional, behavioral, and intellectual—and includes common challenges in each area as well as clues that can help us toward greater levels of skill and understanding in each.

On any kind of journey, it's good to know the tools we're carrying and how to use them. I like to think about the full set of the minor arcana as a kind of user's guide to the human experience, organized into four domains. Through the process of breaking down our experience into these four categories, we can see where our proficiencies and vulnerabilities are. For me personally, more of a thinker by both nature and nurture, I find the secrets of the swords more intuitive to grasp, whereas the cups, which ask us to feel rather than analyze to gain understanding, take work.

Through a visual and symbolic exploration of the four domains, tarot can help us identify the gifts we're most naturally inclined to use as well as the ones we have a harder time with, those we tend to avoid or underutilize. From there, we can make decisions about how to develop competence and skill in all four domains to cultivate greater balance and flexibility.

Wands
Energy

I consider the wands as connected to the energetic domain. In this book, I'll refer to energy as encompassing what doesn't fit neatly into the categories of thoughts, feelings, or behavior. That may be a creative drive, a sense of being here to do something very specific, an inescapable inclination toward engaging the invisible or spiritual, or a physiological experience coupled with intellectual, emotional, or behavioral processes.

As the domain of our experience that evades measurement and quantification, the energetic domain is often neglected or overlooked in evidence-based approaches to healing or change. But it is nonetheless an essential part of the human experience. Being human is more than just a complex interaction between thoughts, feelings, and behavior. Something immeasurable moves us along. Associated with the fire element, the wands have to do with the type of warmth that differentiates the living from the dead. It's here that we learn about accessing, preserving, and protecting the spark of life force energy that drives us along in our particular lives.

The wand has to do with the essential mystery of life, a call to engage with what we may never *know* in the logical ways of knowing that we've grown accustomed to. With one end typically resting on earth and one in the heavens, these magic sticks shed light on the interplay between the material and ethereal, including more practical concerns like cultivating our creative drives and managing the influx and outflow of energy in interpersonal relationships.

Cups
Emotion

Cups are connected to the domain of emotion. We'll approach them this way throughout the book and will also explore them as having to do with relational experiences like connection and intimacy.

Symbolically tied to water, a signifier of life, cups in tarot relate to the stuff that gives life meaning—creativity, imagination, dreaming, connection. As water does, emotion seeks an outlet, and one of the things this suit will show us is the way that emotions evade the neat boundaries that are more easily imposed in the physical domain.

Rarely differentiated entirely from energetic, intellectual, and behavioral experiences, the cups show the ways that emotions can influence behavior and also how, attended to with skill and willingness, they can unlock our own life-bearing and creative potential.

Pentacles
Behavior

Pentacles have traditionally been associated with matters of career and finance but will represent the domain of behavior in this book. We'll define behavior as something we can be seen doing in order to differentiate it from internal actions, like ruminating or accepting. The pentacles are a natural signifier of physical behavior because of their connection with the earth element, the tactile and tangible.

Behavioral therapies—whose emphasis is on behavior change—aim to create awareness and space around the other domains in order to develop the ability to behave in a way that aligns with our values, as opposed to letting thoughts, feelings, and sensations dictate our actions. Sometimes defining our values is the work in itself. As symbols of worth, the pentacles (also known as coins) help us parse out the truly precious from the fool's gold.

Swords
Intellect

The swords are traditionally connected to the psychological domain, and here we'll use them to help us understand the intellectual mind. The intellect, symbolized by the sword with a double edge, gives humans the ability to sort, label, categorize, and separate data into a particular kind of knowledge. But as we will see throughout the suit, this ability has a tendency to get us in trouble.

Many of the sword cards are intensely emotional, a nod to the natural interplay between thoughts and feelings that helps us better understand their dynamic relationship. And perhaps paradoxically, the swords give important secrets about how to use the intellectual mind's double edge for transcending its own divisive tendencies.

How to Use This Book

he practical aim of this book is to provide you with new ways of understanding the tarot based on an attempt to synthesize knowledge from the fields of psychology, behavioral science, spirituality, and old stories. I hope that it will also be a resource for you to better understand your own human experience because, after all, that's what this book of secrets is about. For all self-identified heroes, people on the edge, and mystic way walkers, I hope it will give you a structure—paradoxical as such an endeavor may be—for embracing the unanswerable questions and great mysteries of life.

Each of the seventy-eight cards in the tarot deck can be interpreted from a number of angles and understood in a variety of ways. I've chosen one or two meanings from each and shared accompanying insights and stories drawn from my research, tarot practice, training in social work, and lived experience. This is by no means a book that claims to tell definitively "what the cards mean." To do so would be counter to the overarching message of the Fool's journey, in my view, which resists any fixed meaning and builds the capacity for reality, which is change.

As you'll see in your own work with tarot, the cards whisper secrets through time and depending on context. What follows are some of the secrets they've told me, often in times when I've most needed them. Anyone can develop a relationship with the cards in which they offer what is most needed. I agree with Joseph Campbell's statement that "the person who thinks he has found the ultimate truth is wrong" and assert that the ideas I've shared here are one truth among many.

Though my tarot practice is one that's more exploratory and therapeutic than predictive, I am a lover and practitioner of bibliomancy, a divinatory practice in which you choose a book and flip to a page at random to receive a sacred message or synchronicitous insight. I imagine that this book, which includes Xaviera López's illustrations of all seventy-eight cards in the tarot, could be an awesome tool for such a practice.

Having spent years in self-help book publishing, I can't help but see *Tarot for Change* as more of a self-help book than a how-to guide. My hope in interpreting the cards in the way that I do has always been to convey skills and concepts for living, but to do so in a way that honors the mysteries of life and places us back into a deep mythic context. I hope that this book will both serve as a reminder that you belong and help you claim and step into the particulars of what make you, you.

SECTION II

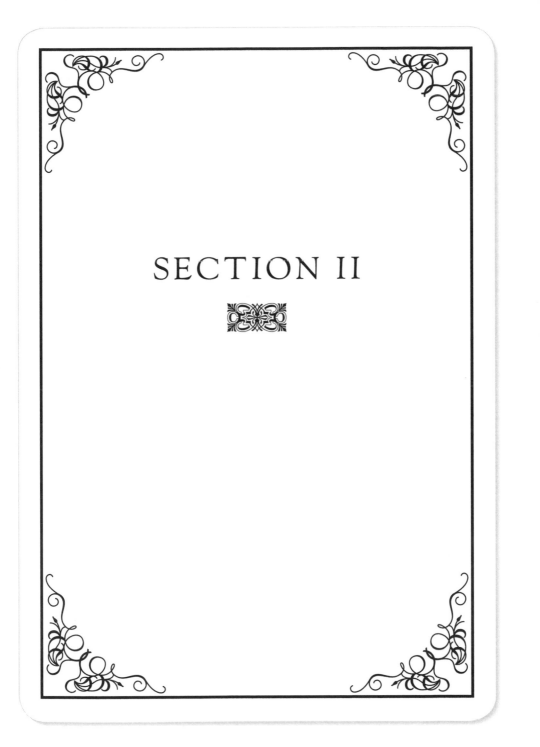

The Major Arcana

The Fool

here's an old story from the Seneca, Indigenous people of the central and western region of what is now called New York State, in which a witch throws a group of men into an ice house in hopes that they'll die inside. But, in mythologist Martin Shaw's telling of the story, the men don't die, because the protagonist in the tale gives the other men this warning: whatever you do, don't sit down on the ice chairs.

So the men dance and sing instead of sitting down, and with the heat that their bodies generate, the hard walls of the ice house start to melt. A patch of sky pokes through the ice house ceiling. Eventually, the sun appears and, with it, the possibility of living to see another day.

Dancing is a bit of a fool's task. You have to get out from beneath the structure of ideas about what's orderly. You have to get okay with looking silly and being misunderstood.

In the study of how people behave, *rule-governed behavior* is a term for action that's taken not because it is the best or right thing to do in a given situation but because a person has begun to do it automatically based on things like social reinforcement, avoidance of discomfort, or a need to feel good all the time.

Rules help us create structure in our lives. But sometimes rules, when followed without question, become like ice houses that trap and freeze us. Inside for too long, we get numb to the naturally occurring contingencies of life that demand flexibility. We're in the ice house any time we say, "This is how it's done, this is how it's always been done, and never mind the fact that it's hurtful, life limiting, and oppressive, or simply doesn't work anymore."

Studies have shown that rigid psychological rules contribute to mental health issues. For example, if you have a rule that you can consume only a certain number of calories each day, that rule can lead to compensatory and sometimes destructive behaviors when that limit has been exceeded. Or if you have a rule that says being sad is bad and therefore should be avoided at all costs, you might use alcohol, sex, drugs, or shopping to numb any and all feelings of melancholy.

Many spiritual and religious traditions teach aspirants to always be kind to strangers, misfits, and outcasts because they may be gods in disguise. Myths and old stories reveal a link between the Fool—a misfit and rule breaker—and wisdom and holiness. Though many knights sought hard after the Holy Grail, it was Percival—who began as a wannabe riding a donkey and wearing an ill-fitting uniform—who found it. Latvian poet Robert Avens wrote that jesters in old stories symbolize imagination, a capacity to see through the emperor's clothes, to melt an ice house that would otherwise be "intolerable in its sheer and uninterrupted pomposity."

In Aleister Crowley and Lady Frieda Harris's Thoth tarot, the Fool is illustrated as the pagan mythological green man, the personification of springtime. He is the one with the courage to break through the frozen ground of winter when the time comes for flowers, to challenge the structure of the day in service of new life. As David Steindl-Rast wrote, "Though life (over and over again) creates structures, structures do not create life."

Change at any level—the personal, relational, cultural, systemic—requires two things: that we be courageous enough to dance weirdly in the frozen spaces and that we be willing to feel whatever angst or uncertainty that brings. I want to give a charm here for any aspiring fools and hopeful walkers of the weird, rule-breaking way: The job of rules is to manage; they serve a function of control. In a community, rules control the social climate. In an individual, rules control the internal environment, which includes thoughts, feelings, and sensations. So when you break a rule, expect to be met by a wild chorus of thoughts, feelings, and sensations that the ice house walls were doing a great job of keeping out. Know this when you start dancing, and you'll be better equipped for what comes next.

The Magician

In order to understand the Magician, we first need to understand magic. My favorite definition of magic comes from the anonymous author of *Meditations on the Tarot*, who writes that "all magic… is the putting into practice of this: that the subtle rules the dense." It is from this definition that I've determined healing to be a magical process, and from which I've begun to understand behavior change, specifically—something that once sounded mundane to me—as miraculous.

The Magician has four tools on his workbench: the wand, the cup, the pentacle, and the sword. These tools symbolize the four domains of the human experience—energy, emotion, behavior, and thoughts, respectively—three of which are subtle (energy, emotion, thoughts) and one which is dense (behavior). Energy, feelings, and thoughts are subtle because they are interior and invisible. Behavior, that which a person can be seen doing, is dense because it is exterior. It has to do with the tangible, material reality.

If magic is using the subtle to influence the dense, any process that involves using the invisible "subtle" aspects of our experience (energy, emotions, thoughts) to influence the visible "dense" ones (behavior and physical reality) qualifies as magic. The act of taking something you may have once believed to hold little value—like grief, rage, despair, social anxiety—and using it to move toward something precious is a kind of modern-day alchemy.

Therapists use terms like *radical acceptance* and *post-traumatic growth* to describe the work of taking adverse experiences and using them to grow. Through my years in self-help book publishing, I've rarely experienced such clinical terms as adequate for the processes they're meant to describe. I'd say words like *miracles* and *magic* are a better fit.

All of us are born into fertile conditions for magic because of the operating system we're given at birth, whose primary mode is this: secure as much pleasure as possible for the least amount of discomfort. If you are unaware that this program is running, behavior is mostly habit and machination. Everything from the route you take to get to work to the events you attend to the things you consume is performed with the underlying aim of attaining maximum enjoyment at the cheapest cost. The author of *Meditations on the Tarot* wrote that anything done from this mode is not really *done* at all, in fact, it just happens. Automatically, unconsciously, and *unmagically*.

In acceptance and commitment therapy, or ACT, the first task is often to clarify personal values. This is an internal process, which is to say that it is a subtle one. It involves identifying that which is precious, which includes a certain degree of discernment—using the sword's double edge to parse what's real from what isn't. Our true values emerge from the invisible domains of our drives and desires—concerns related to the wand and cup. Having engaged the subtle domains, then comes the magic. You take what you know about what's precious and make a commitment to behaving in alignment with that even if it means going against the program of securing the most pleasure for the least effort.

When we do the opposite of what our programming tells us to do, we cross the threshold from the habitual to the magical. Referring to the biblical teaching "love your enemies, do good to those who hate you, bless those who curse you," the author of *Meditations on the Tarot* writes that this is wisdom straight from a "school for the miraculous." Anytime you do something that breaks from the operating system of maximum pleasure for minimal discomfort, you're doing magic. You're stepping into the psychic template of the Magician archetype and performing a miracle.

Sometimes the Magician is interpreted as representing the conscious mind, in contrast to the High Priestess, guardian of the unconscious. Physics teaches us that objects will move in the same direction and speed that they were going unless they are intervened upon by something. When it comes to our habits, there are many ways to intervene. In most cases, we have to be aware of them first. Catherine Mac-Coun writes that "when our unconscious will is stronger than our conscious intention.... It is unmagical." In other words, when we live without examining the whys or hows of our particular lives, we are living by laws of meaninglessness, not magic. From this perspective, becoming conscious is the first step to performing miracles. As Jungian analyst Marie-Louise von Franz wrote, "Becoming conscious of something presupposes a choice." And so that awareness is step one, as is the Magician on the path of the twenty-two major secrets.

The High Priestess

I t's tempting to believe that simply refusing to speak something aloud is a sure way to keep a secret, but the truth is that secrets tell themselves in all kinds of ways. They're spoken in the choices we make, how we hold our bodies, what we do with our hands and feet, and the ways we behave toward others and ourselves.

Behavior is also a language, and when we start to view it this way, we can see how things swallowed and tamped down have the tenacity of water in their drive to find throughways. We begin to see that even when we haven't moved our mouths and made a sound, we still speak. And that the people around us are listening, affected by what they hear. Even if the message comes out scrambled or distorted, and even if those not fluent in the language of behavior have to really strain their ears to understand, you can trust the message is felt somehow. Come closer. Go away. I hate you. Don't leave me. I want this. I am scared of this. I'm ready to change. I want to stay the same.

Trauma therapist Laurie Kahn has written about how unprocessed trauma appears in code. She writes, "Stories unshared don't disappear; they return in relationships, silently taking prisoners. If the trauma remains unknown, unspoken, and unconscious, it does harm." Our secrets and unconscious fears have their own ways of revealing themselves, and we can decode them by looking at the choices we make in how we behave.

Years ago I was receiving a tarot reading and the High Priestess appeared in the spread. After much discussion of the issue I'd brought, the reader asked simply, "What about this issue is not being said?" I knew immediately. There was an unclaimed desire that I'd been omitting from my narrative to myself, her, and everyone involved. My choices were telling on me, and the reader was fluent enough in the language of behavior to hear it. My actions revealed that I wanted the complete opposite of what I was saying. Until that moment, I hadn't been ready to own that.

The High Priestess sits at the threshold of that moment when you realize you should be listening. Listening not just for words, listening in a different way than you have been. Rachel Pollack writes that the Magician and High Priestess represent an original splitting, between the conscious and unconscious. The unconscious is that which runs counter to conscious awareness, so it's slippery by nature, but when you see the High Priestess in a spread, the card is often an indicator that something in the room is either not being said or may require a bit of decoding.

Of course, not all secrets need to be spoken aloud. Just because something is true doesn't necessarily make it palatable, as anyone carrying an unspeakable truth knows. Suppression, repression, and tight lips are defenses that make living under the weight of the unspeakable a possibility even if it isn't ideal. But recognizing the ways that these things influence our lives and choices is also protective. Because when we do not acknowledge our secrets, they tend to express themselves in ways that undermine our free will. Maybe some stories can only be told in the language of behavior, and maybe here it is also possible for them to be heard, honored, and reconciled if needed.

The Empress

I spent the first year of my daily yoga practice oscillating between the postures I was supposed to be doing and crying in child's pose. I was twenty-four then, and after more than two decades of habitually leaving my body, when I began the titrated journey home—coming in and then leaving, in and then leaving—I was met with waves of intense emotions that had been lying latent, waiting to be acknowledged. It was as if they'd been sitting by the window of my abandoned body-house, watching the driveway, hopeful at first, perking up at the flash of a headlight or any sign of my return, but growing increasingly hostile as the years passed. Shooting daggers out the window and gnashing their teeth. *How dare she stay gone for so long.*

What I'd been able to process before that time through journaling, talk therapy, and other forms of meaning making had been a start for sure, but there was so much more that simply needed to be felt to be released.

Energy healer Donna Eden writes that "becoming civilized is, to a large extent, learning not to do what your body wants you to do," which resonates. In our culture we are conditioned to prize intellectual knowing and neglect intuitive or body knowing. We are taught that science alone is real and that other ways of knowing are fantastical or unreliable.

The Empress represents nature and is, in my experience, one of the most misunderstood arcana in the tarot. People love her but can't put a finger on why. I think it's that we long to be in our bodies but have forgotten how, and she shows us what it would feel like if we could.

Many of us think of the wild as something "out there," and I think that's sad for us. It shows how cut off we are from the fact that somewhere deep down and old we are still the wild, and the body—with all its cycles and rhythms and ebbs and flows and generation and degeneration—is proof.

Because many of us grew up in homes where learning to regulate emotions and tolerate distress wasn't part of the culture or curriculum, we instead learned the habit of dissociating to cope, simply leaving the body when it becomes too much to be there. We return for moments here and there, but when it gets scary, we leave. We leave by drinking, shopping, scrolling our phones, having sex with people we don't feel safe with, and any number of other exit strategies. We numb in whatever way we can because that's our best strategy for dealing. But ultimately it never helps, because numbing is not healing.

During my first year of graduate school I was hired to write a story about yoga and addiction recovery for a popular women's magazine. I knew from my own experience that yoga was a powerful tool in recovery, but I didn't know why and was excited to learn more about the mechanics of healing. One of the people I spoke to during my research was neuroscientist and researcher Sat Bir Singh Khalsa, a professor at Harvard Medical School who had developed a theory about why yoga was so helpful for those recovering from drug and alcohol addiction.

He told me that yoga helps people develop mind-body awareness—which is something I suspect we come into this world with but that gets chipped away as we get older and integrate into the structures of our particular cultures. Khalsa said mind-body awareness, which is developed through a practice of directing one's attention back to the body, helps people to remember what feels good and what doesn't.

When we aren't in the body, we're not able to experience the consequences of behavior that disrupts our energy and lives. We push through hangovers; ignore hunger and fullness cues; hang out too much with people whom we don't feel good around; spend years, decades, and sometimes lifetimes doing work that elicits agony or, perhaps worse, nothing at all.

Khalsa said that the best motivator for behavior change is from the bottom up, meaning that coming into the body and actually feeling the impacts of a particular behavior will give us everything we need to know about whether to keep doing it or not. In order to access this information, though, we have to be willing to go back to the place where it lives: the body. Joseph Campbell said it beautifully: "The mind can ramble off in strange ways and want things that the body does not want.... Myths and rites were means of putting the mind in accord with the body and the way of life in accord with the way that nature dictates."

More than any other motivator for change—knowing the harmful effects, reading statistics, even knowing intellectually that certain behaviors are messing with your dearest relationships—the capacity to experience how something *truly* feels may be one of the most important skills for change.

The Emperor

I f I think back to every time I've acted on an impulse to do something that felt urgent, like it just *had* to be done and which I felt powerless to *not* do, I see a terrified person doing anything she can to regain a sense of control.

What I've observed about compulsions over the years, in myself and in others, is that they're often a reaction to feeling powerless. The compulsive behavior is how, in the absence of a better way, we regain a sense of agency. So there are two issues underlying compulsivity as I see it: we can't tolerate our lack of control, and in the process of trying to manage that intolerance, we often create more problems for ourselves.

That sense of powerlessness is often triggered by other people's behavior. Someone is doing something that we don't want them to do and our lack of control over the situation stimulates a sense of terror in us. And in that moment we mistake that small scared part of us as the whole of who we are. Sometimes it's triggered by an internal event, an emotion that feels so big and so overwhelming—a deep terror of being left behind or rejected, maybe—that threatens to swallow us whole. Without a better way to deal with these kinds of experiences, we act out in ways that might ultimately make things worse but that at least grant a fleeting sense of power. It's interesting how, in moments of uncertainty, we tend to prioritize a sense of control over almost everything. And it's hugely problematic for so many of us.

The anonymous author of *Meditations on the Tarot* wrote of this card that "where there is authority... there compulsion is superfluous" and that the Emperor is not only a figure of power but a renunciant. In

51

other words, the person who embodies true authority must renounce something. More specifically, the author writes that the person must renounce compulsion and violence, two forces that may give a false sense of authority but are the mark of someone who has no real personal power to speak of. So while compulsive behavior is an exercise in violence against ourselves and others, in which we forcefully fight away what we fear, true authority is marked by a degree of behavioral sovereignty—the ability to choose actions with intention and care, even when we feel scared and powerless.

A person who holds true power is one who is able to occupy spaces of intense uncertainty, and all the feelings that brings up, while remaining stable in their actions, that is, renouncing one's need to react in a way that will give them a false sense of control.

The Emperor is the fourth card of the major arcana and the number four is associated with grounding, like the four corners of a house or a table. Make your body into a house or a table when you feel afraid. A house whose walls can stand still to witness many, many things, the joys and the terrors, with thick oak floors sturdy enough to bear the weight. See whether, the next time you feel overwhelmed with a feeling or thought pattern that's telling you to do something that will betray your own interests, you can be still. Even if it's just for five minutes. That's how you practice power.

The Hierophant

hen I was in the early stages of writing this book, someone left a copy of *Meditations on the Tarot: A Journey into Christian Hermeticism* in the entryway to the studio where I was practicing yoga every morning. I wasn't sure I really needed another tarot book, especially one like this, seven hundred pages long and covering only the major arcana. But at the time I was also in the process of preparing to teach my first class on psychological applications of the major arcana, and I figured it couldn't hurt to at least thumb through the book.

The following week I spent Thanksgiving alone, preparing for the class. Totally uninspired by my existing analyses of the Hierophant, I picked up the mysterious book I'd found and flipped to the chapter about the fifth major arcana, titled in the book as in the Tarot de Marseilles: "The Pope."

The book describes the Hierophant as first and foremost a card about benediction and prayer. The author writes about spiritual practice as an exercise of *vertical respiration*—where one forges and continuously maintains a connection between above and below. Spiritual practice, by this understanding, is engaging in two-way conversation with a Higher Power. You say a prayer and you wait for the response. You breathe out and then in. I'd been praying a lot at that time that I would receive the guidance I needed to write my first book.

I've noticed that people tend to secularize the Hierophant or interpret it with a degree of hostility, given its associations with organized religion and the experiences people have inside such institutions. Many times in one-on-one readings I've wrestled with how to translate this card into a secret that would be less spiritual, knowing that people come to me for my decidedly "practical" or "down-to-earth" way of interpreting the cards.

But no matter how far we may swing—individually or culturally— toward the pragmatic and scientific, we remain spiritual, meaning-making beings with an inclination toward the numinous. And even if we choose to work with the major arcana for their more exoteric or everyday applications, these cards will always remain a map for a quest toward truth, toward union with the Absolute. The Hierophant is and must be symbolic of spiritual life, of the engagement with and interpretation of the sacred, that which transcends the material realm.

One of the reasons I think people shy away from spiritual practice is that we are rewards-driven beings living in a culture of instant gratification. There are a lot of ways we could understand a card like the Hierophant that could offer more immediate implications for daily life, such as the popular view of the card as having to do with education, indoctrination, and conformity with social structures. We all have ideas and beliefs that we ought to examine and question so that we can stay true to who we are. Certainly, if you need an invitation to do so, let this be it. But it feels important, still, to carve out a place for the significance of spirituality, however unfashionable.

Many psychological problems are rooted in our experience of self—how well or how poorly developed it is, how bounded or porous, how solid or shame based. Our sense of self has profound impacts on the most important area of life, our relationships. Spiritual practice is a way of practicing relationships; it's how we position ourselves as at once important and not all-powerful. When we open the lines of communication between the self and something greater, we position ourselves to recall that we have a voice in things, but never the final say. This might feel frightening at first, but it can also be a relief. Because it takes a bit off the plate of who we understand as "I" and opens us up to input from something beyond the sphere of our own influence. Even if your spiritual practice is just recognizing in some way, each day, that there are things unfolding that you have no say in, that's a way of honoring something greater.

Spiritual practice is how many people in the throes of intense psychological conflict learn to surrender, accept, and be willing. Opening up our awareness to a larger, mysterious order of things is a way to let go of our efforts to control the outcomes in our lives and to listen for answers that emerge from a process that has nothing to do with us personally. In understanding this, when things don't work out, we don't automatically assume it to be an indication of our worth or lovability or competence. We don't have to interpret every uncertain or undesirable circumstance as our problem to fix. At the very least, this gives us grace when things don't go our way.

The Lovers

here are so many good secrets tucked into the tarot, but for these reflections, I've chosen the meanings that felt both juiciest and most practical. After all, what's juicier than something you can inject directly into your everyday life?

Some traditional interpretations of the Lovers say that it's about choice, while popular folk interpretations use the card to indicate a significant romantic relationship in the querent's life. Pamela Colman Smith's illustration in the Rider-Waite deck features an angel overlooking two people in a garden, which hints that the card is also about love as a spiritual exercise. In the experience of union with another person, we get a taste of something that transcends life's separations—the mystic's ideal of a return to wholeness.

I've noticed that exploring romantic love as a spiritual practice doesn't always resonate with people, but understanding *choice* in the context of romantic relationships, as an opportunity for personal evolution, almost always does. I, for one, see personal growth as inherently spiritual—connected to and pulled along by something greater— but however you like to think about it or whatever language you use to get there is good.

I think a lot of us, at least until we know different, choose lovers based on learned relationship dynamics. Perhaps we grew up in enmeshed environments so we pick people with bad boundaries who expect too much and give too little because that feels like home. Or we're used to holding in our disappointments because sharing them invited criticism and punishment in our families, so we choose lovers who are equally if not more unsafe to share with. We tend to choose the energetics we're familiar with, even when they hurt.

We didn't get to choose what we learned about love as children, but as adults it's different. We can pick lovers based on the things we want to learn in relationships, like how to receive or how to be vulnerable. We can do the old laundry list of qualities we want a future lover to have but we can also make lists about the ways we want to learn and grow in love. To receive, to be vulnerable, to be like the scent of home to someone, to take the sweet with the bitter, to prioritize the needs of a whole.

A generous lover could surely help us practice receiving even when doing so strikes terror in our hearts and every ounce of our being wants to say, "No thank you, send this back." Or maybe we want to learn how to speak up when our hearts are frightened or disappointed, rather than bottle things up and wait to pop knowing explosions erode closeness over time. In that case, a lover whose heart is a safe room to say "I'm hurt by this" without punishment would be good. Or if we wish to find better ways of coping with our fears of abandonment, then we could date someone who we like so much it scares us.

Another reason viewing romantic relationships this way is good is that by the logic that all lovers bring lessons, when we choose lovers who teach us things we really don't want to learn—like about our own bad boundaries, our flimsy sense of self, our compulsive overextending, our insecurity, and so on—we don't have to see it as a reflection of our brokenness or inadequacy in love but rather as a testament to our ability to find the exact teachers we need at the precise time we need them. That feels better and more empowering, I think.

So it seems worthwhile, when preparing to enter into a partnership or union, to consider: What lessons and skills am I ready to learn? And instead of asking, Is this person right for me? we could ask, Is this person someone with whom I can learn the lessons I am wanting and ready to learn, and then some I don't see yet?

Willfully enrolling in the lessons we most deeply need is a frightening prospect, but it is worthwhile. As Clarissa Pinkola Estés wrote, "To love pleasure takes little. To love truly takes a hero who can manage his own fear." And this is also the choice that the Lovers gives us: Do we continue to go about according to our misunderstandings about love and outdated relational blueprints? Or do we learn to go beyond them, not only so that life can be more pleasant, but also so that we can have new skills for going to the places that scare us?

The Chariot

feel like I'm constantly doing damage control with people I work with around unlearning the myth of willpower as some sort of magic pill or panacea. I grew up with an Italian American father and watched a lot of *Rocky* movies as a kid, so I get it. I, too, have wanted to believe that with hard work and elbow grease I could have what I wanted. Robert Bly wrote, "Always cry for what you want," and I took that to heart. But what I didn't do, and what no one around me seemed to be doing, either, was spend time learning to manage what happens when life tells you no.

I'm not knocking willpower. It's a really perfect tool for certain challenges. Like external ones, where you have some amount of control over outcomes, such as passing a test or training to run a race. But willpower is not so helpful when it comes to internal challenges, like social anxiety or grief. In fact, the way willpower usually manifests in those kinds of cases is through the exertion of efforts to push away or dull the feelings you don't want. And that gets ugly fast.

Willpower can take us only so far, and when we hit that limit, it can feel as though the vehicle we were driving doesn't work anymore. The wheels spin and we don't move. We're not sure how to get out, and even if we were, we have no other modes of transportation. We'd walk, but our legs are set inside two tons of cement.

The obstacle course of achievement under capitalism isn't built to teach pathfinding, it's built to teach compliance with a preset path. To an extent, you do get to pick your own adventure, but you'll be told what you need to do to get the prize, as well as what the prize is or ought to be. Life isn't some obstacle course that you're meant to muscle your way through, with rows of neatly arranged blocks and barricades. It's just that this particular environment has trained us to think that it is, or that it should be.

Where willpower may have worked well for you to get through the obstacle course of your schooling, or the career path you chose before you had any idea your life wasn't just an extension clipped onto someone else's definition of success, the moment you decide you want to do something different with your life is the moment you realize you're going to need a new set of skills, ones for navigation and way finding.

In dialectical behavior therapy there's a thing called *willfulness*, which is similar to willpower but generally considered a liability. Willfulness is when you impose your will on reality, which is fine in some cases but harmful when reality simply cannot be what you want. We're given many stories from the time we're young about the value of willpower and pushing through obstacles, but we're not given stories about what happens when we hit concrete walls, when we do not get what we want no matter how loud we cry, and when willpower is the wrong skill for the circumstance. We aren't really set up to fail well. Rather, we're indoctrinated with the value of persevering and refusing to take no for an answer.

But life is both yeses and nos. We don't get what we want all the time. It sounds so juvenile and so obvious, and yet so many of us really struggle with accepting that. And sometimes, and this is something I've always thought about with the Chariot—which is popularly read as a card about success but depicts a man with his legs cemented into a vehicle—we do get what we thought we wanted, only to realize it's a trap and now we feel hopelessly stuck. Then what?

The Chariot has never said much to me about the "then what." I think its medicine is more in the way it reveals the limitations of willpower and the dangers of believing life is simply a series of completing difficult tasks and yoking wild bulls so they'll do what we want them to do. That just isn't at all what this is. I wish we'd tell more than only the stories where we struggle and then get what we want, as if always getting what we want were the point of life. How silly, how childish, how one-note and unmagical. Yes, willpower can carry you to many places. But make no mistake, stuckness is one of them.

Strength

trength has always been about self-compassion for me. A woman encounters a lion; a gentle and wise part of us meets a wild, ferocious part; there is curiosity, kindness, and respect. This is the dynamic that self-compassion creates as we encounter the things about ourselves we don't like and remind ourselves that we are human.

Mythologist Joseph Campbell dedicated his life to old stories from around the world and identified themes and phases that were common to each. Part of the value in that is that it helps us see which aspects of our experiences may be shared human experiences and which are unique to our contexts and temperaments.

One theme that Campbell noticed in stories the world over was the reaching of an initiatory threshold. After a hero had heard the call to adventure, sometimes denied the call, and finally answered it, they would set out and soon reach the first threshold, a portal toward the destination that was always guarded by a dreadful being of some kind. In myths, threshold guardians take the shape of ogres who induce panic, serpents who seduce and then kill, and benevolent lotus-eaters who share feasts of flowers that sedate all those who eat them.

The ogres and serpents and lotus-eaters who guard the thresholds of great quests probably represent internal gatekeepers more than external ones—anxiety, self-doubt, unworthiness, lust, laziness, to name a few. In the model of acceptance and commitment therapy, the aim of treatment is to build psychological flexibility, which is the ability to move in the direction of one's values even in the face of internal obstacles. In mythic terms, this kind of flexibility is basically the ability of the hero to hear the call, answer it, and not be pulled off the path by any ogre, serpent, or lotus-eater.

The forest-dwelling Arcadian god Pan, for example, is a gatekeeper who induces panic in those who wish to cross him. A swift death is brought to all who attempt to outrun him, but those who find a way to pay their respects and honor him as they enter his domain are blessed. With his powers, he then ensures that their crops yield abundant bounty and that their health is good.

Strength is called Force in some decks. Heroes in myths across cultures who are able to use the forces within them—such as humility, curiosity, and kindness—to pass by threshold guardians give an important lesson: We cannot rely on the deployment of willpower and *brute* force in the face of internal gatekeepers. When facing guardians like anxiety, self-doubt, or a harsh inner critic, we're more likely to find that attempts to outrun, hide from, deny, or even destroy them is a path toward grave danger and deep trouble.

But when we learn to honor the humanity in these difficult experiences—anger, grief, loneliness, despair, guilt, shame—we discover that they cannot "kill" us, nor can they pull us from our paths. We honor them by paying our respects, summoning willingness, being curious, and engaging a genuine desire to understand.

The Hermit

One of the most amazing things for me during the process of researching and writing this book was finding confirmation for what I perceived in my early days of studying tarot—that the secrets tucked into these cards radiate the wisdoms of both ancient philosophies and contemporary evidence-based therapies. And that while there are important distinctions, there are also real philosophical overlaps between the philosophies of the ancient Egyptians and Greeks, the Catholicism that I grew up with, the Taoism and Buddhism that I became curious about as a teenager, and the psychotherapy models that I trained in during graduate school.

The ninth major secret, the Hermit, is often interpreted as relating to the peace and prudence that come from walking what Buddhists call the Middle Path. In the words of Buddhist monk Ajahn Chah, "You see both sides, so you have peace. If you only see one side, there is suffering. Once you see both sides, then you follow the Middle Way. This is the right practice of the mind. This is what we call 'straightening out our understanding.'" The lesson of the Hermit, the spiritual aspirant, is learning to dwell inside liminal space between extremes, because poles are illusory by nature and breed suffering.

The Christian version of a middle way might be the middle point that's formed by the two lines of the crucifix, which brings together cerebral intellectuality and spontaneous spirituality. In dialectical behavior therapy, it might be the "wise mind" space where our emotional and rational minds link and we can draw a bit from each to formulate our knowing, because too much logic or too much emotion creates a distorted understanding and, thereby, suffering. And in Western esotericism, Hermeticism specifically, the middle way is the ideal of the "totality of things." Where nothing is black or white, this or that; all seeming opposites are identical in nature, different only in degree.

Though behavioral scientists might be reluctant to associate themselves with the Western mystery traditions, both the ideals of the Hermit and the DBT therapist aim to walk the peaceful path between worlds, a space that surpasses the limited paradigm of either/or and moves into the world of both/and. The therapist who asks, "Can both of those things be true at once?" is activating the hermit archetype whether they're doing so consciously or not.

Both the Hermit and the practitioner of DBT understand that peace is not available in the land of opposites. To the extent that we see things in terms of this or that, black or white, him or her, above or below, or within or without, peace evades us. Coming to this understanding is the aim of the Fool's journey toward the World, just as it is that of the person learning to overcome what's called all-or-nothing or black-and-white thinking in therapy. Whether we're digging into ancient Buddhist texts or a DBT manual, we are let in on the secret that peace exists in a middle way, in a state of wise mind, in the synthesis of opposites.

The anonymous author of *Meditations on the Tarot* wrote of the Hermit:

> It is the heart which is simultaneously active and contemplative, untiringly and unceasingly. It walks. It walks day and night, and we listen day and night to the steps of its incessant walking. This is why, if we want to represent a man who lives the law of the heart, who is centred in the heart and is a visible expression of the heart—the "wise and good father," or the Hermit—we present him as walking, steadily and without haste.

Many years later, psychologist and founder of DBT Marsha Linehan wrote, on the state of wise mind, the aim of her therapy:

Wise mind is that part of each person that can know and experience truth.... It has a certain peace.... Wise mind is like having a heart, everyone has one, whether they experience it or not.

Just as the World in tarot isn't a fixed place, but rather a flux state that one comes in and out of through time, the peaceful middle way isn't a static space or destination. It's not the type of place where you arrive, stay, and hold residence. There, too, is yet another temptation to impose oppositional thinking: I am either there, or I am not there. Healed or still broken. This is why in many decks the Hermit is pictured walking; a metaphor for the way of a person who is at peace with the flux state of reality. That is, changing and being stuck, expanding and contracting, evolving and devolving, living and dying.

Wheel of Fortune

hile I was in social work school, I learned about the stages of change model, which was developed by James Prochaska and Carlo DiClemente to support people in recovery as a way to normalize and put into context the experiences common to the different phases of change. The model posits that change often begins with precontemplation, which is before you know that change needs to be made, and moves from there to contemplation, preparation, action, and ultimately through to maintenance, which is after the change has been made and you have to adjust to your new life. The model even includes relapse, which the authors believed to be a natural and normal part of the recovery process.

"Change" is one of the most popularly used interpretations of the Wheel of Fortune that I've found, and mythic representations of the wheel often support this as its message. In Roman mythology the goddess Fortuna had the power to bestow both glory and decrepitude, an ancient way of understanding the natural phenomena of chance and change. Myths and old stories give us metaphors and symbols to help us remember how our ancestors made sense of enduring realities, but our own life experiences also give us all we need in order to know the inevitability of change. Change is a thing we have no real choice but to accept and, ideally, find grace in. It's one of those things in life that is just happening, regardless. As certain as the sun is going to rise and set sometime within the next twenty-four hours of your reading this.

I'm not big on advice like "trust the process," because it's idealistic, not realistic. We don't trust the process and that's our problem. So much of what gets us in trouble is our lack of faith in any process where we're not in control, and our total rejection of any and all forces that dare to override the way we were hoping things would go from our limited vantage point. That minuscule vista where a single spoke meets the rim of this great wheel we live in.

We all get that we *should* trust the process by now, and a good deal of us even understand why. But the simple fact remains that we do not know how. And I certainly don't know all the way how to, either, but I do think that Prochaska and DiClemente were onto something with their stages of change model. Especially the relapse part they built into it, a nod to the fact that no matter how hard you work or how good your intentions, with a flick of the wrist Fortuna can spin that wheel and send you back to square one.

The Wheel of Fortune is a symbol of change and it's also a symbol of evolution; its circular shape symbolizes the marriage of opposites, the *totality of things*. Though we tend to think of evolution as a continuously upward trajectory (shout-out to the March of Progress diagram, which depicts the ascent of humans from primate to man), the Wheel of Fortune reminds us that to evolve could be more accurately described as a process of both contraction and expansion.

A caterpillar's metamorphosis, for instance, *requires* a cocoon before a butterfly. Yes, this is an overused metaphor for change, but it bears repeating, because a cocoon is not a thing that *sometimes* happens before a butterfly. It is a thing that always, absolutely and irrevocably, happens. A prerequisite. I think that it's easier to trust a process when you understand how it works. This way, instead of panicking and being like, "Oh f*ck, what's happening," you might be able to say something more like "Wow this is awful, and part of the process, and temporary." And really mean it.

I like the latter better because I think it's more helpful. And notice how it brings together two seemingly conflicted realities; the stage is both awful and necessary. Life is simply not as clear-cut as the mind makes it out to be.

It's common in old stories for heroes to be given a charm to protect them on their paths by a helper of some kind—an old woman who lives in the forest, a hermit, a king's daughter who favors the hero. So if you've pulled the Wheel of Fortune or are working with it, here's a charm that I'd like you to have: not everything that feels bad is wrong. And when you're breaking an old pattern or doing something different, it's very common to feel worse before you feel better. You were doing something the old way because the old way let you avoid things that scared you. And when you break free of this old pattern, every monster, demon, and terrifying thing is going to show up, and the thing that once protected you can't do that anymore.

And counterintuitive as it may be, if you're passing through those low points on the wheel, it's a sure sign you're moving.

Justice

here's an old Irish tale of five sons who stop at a well while traveling. They are thirsty, but the well is guarded by an old woman whom Standish O'Grady describes in his telling of the story as "variously unwholesome... [with] warped crooked shins garnished with massive ankles and a pair of capacious shovels; knotty knees she had, and livid nails." The woman says she will gladly give the young men water, but only if they give her a kiss. One by one, the men recoil in disgust, opting for dehydration over having to make contact with something they see as hideous.

That is, until the young son Niall makes his request for water. When asked for a kiss, he eagerly says yes and, not only that, agrees to lie down (which I'm pretty sure means have sex) with her. He leans in for the kiss and when his lips touch hers, she transforms into a woman who meets the beauty standards of the day and place: "She had lustrous teeth of pearl, mouth red as the rowanberry.... 'a galaxy of charms.'"

When asked who she is, the woman replies, "Royal Rule."

Where I live, we misunderstand the word *justice*. We use it to talk about systems of punishment, vengeance, and retribution, rarely imagining it as having to do with healing and restoration. One of the functions of stories—and other things written in the language of metaphor, archetype, and symbol—is that they can remind us of what underlies the words we use, because while words can clarify, they can also obscure. Stories and symbols bring us back to a time and place when concepts like justice were a reflection of naturally occurring processes observed in the world and attributed to gods and other fantastical beings beyond the sphere of human influence. Folktales like the one about the Irish brothers have often depicted justice as a natural law that rewards the gentle and kindhearted. Not necessarily to say, "Do good and good will follow," but rather to solidify the link between action and consequence.

Justice in tarot, which is called Adjustment in the Thoth deck, asks questions about cause and effect as well as lessons learned. In compassion-focused therapy (CFT), which uses theories of evolutionary psychology to put into context the experiences of modern humans, our neuroses—anxiety, for example—aren't viewed as defects but simply traits that have evolved over the course of human history to keep us safe in response to environmental threats. Anger, for example, may have evolved as a social bargaining tool to help us avoid being wronged over and over again. Shame likely evolved to encourage prosocial behavior among groups in service of solidarity and cohesion, without which our species would not have survived.

The same can be said of the less than desirable traits and behaviors in our individual life history.

When we make the space to reflect on why we do what we do, we often come to realize that it all made sense once. To understand something is to validate it, and when we can validate, we're living in alignment with the royal rule of compassionate living.

Clarissa Pinkola Estés has remarked that in old stories, those who are gentle with what is undesirable or ugly are many times blessed, while those who scorn and reject ugliness are either barred from their desires or punished, often cruelly. This lesson can be applied to how we to respond to things about ourselves we don't like. Justice teaches us that when we're cold and rejecting toward the things in ourselves that we find grotesque and undesirable, that attitude yields consequences just as it would if we were to treat a friend that way: loss of trust, dignity, and personal power. On the other hand, when we practice kindness and willingness to engage with the parts of ourselves that we view as hideous or unlovable, we're bound to receive a benediction. It could be anything from a moment of peace free from the reign of the harsh inner critic to significant and lasting change. And it's important to remember that we don't have to love or even like ourselves to be kind.

When we begin to see that what we once viewed as fatally flawed or irredeemably defective is a natural consequence of having come up in the environment we did, we create spaciousness from the urge to punish or berate ourselves and call it justice. Paradoxically, understanding and validation act like magic charms that help us carve out the openings we need to make adjustments.

The Hanged Man

he Hanged Man is a card that a lot of people hate getting because it's often read as an instruction to suspend action and assume a posture of passivity, which we not only loathe the thought of but also have no idea *how* to do. It's not our fault that such a directive is frustrating; our brains have literally evolved for problem-solving, and our ability to take action when something feels off or upside down is what's helped us survive as a species.

Truly, it goes against our nature to "wait and see" when we're in a situation we'd rather not be in. When you're disoriented and unable to tell which side is up, you're evolutionarily designed to figure a way out of there. But with its image of a man hanging upside down, this card whispers secrets of a perspective shift, the flipping of an assumption on its head. Let's start with the assumption that suspending physical action means doing nothing.

For so long the idea of acceptance confounded me because I felt like it was a thing I needed to let happen to me rather than a thing I could actively do. Steven Hayes, a behavioral scientist and one of the founders of a therapy constructed entirely on the value of acceptance—called acceptance and commitment therapy, or ACT—writes that "acceptance is not passive tolerance or resignation but an intentional behavior that alters the function of inner experiences from events to be avoided to a focus of interest, curiosity, and observation."

I personally find the idea of acceptance as an action very soothing, because when we're in times of uncertainty or confusion, the reality is that most of us would prefer to do something about it. Again, this isn't because we're hopeless neurotics or control freaks but because thousands of years of human evolution have selected for a certain degree of proactive problem-solving. But what does it really mean to "do something" or to "take action"?

Maybe the very assumption that action is something that happens only visibly and in the external world is problematic. Because when you think about it, there's actually a whole lot you can do that's invisible. You can sit back and take a look at a difficult emotion with curiosity. You can make yourself large enough to hold fiery rage without striking out or melting. You can extend validation to yourself when your critical inner voice is going off. You can sit with discomfort, taking note of its taste and texture.

I mean, do you really think the Hanged Man isn't having thoughts, feelings, sensations all strung up and upside down like that? Having spent years getting to know him and seeing him in all kinds of contexts, I've come to think it's whatever he's doing that's invisible to the naked eye that gave him that halo around his head.

Death

I n her iconic book *Women Who Run with the Wolves*, Clarissa Pinkola Estés wrote about the life-death-life cycle: everything that lives dies, and what dies also lives. We understand the first part, at least intellectually, though it doesn't stop us from suffering in our losses. But the second part we still tend to forget about: what dies, lives. To say that "what dies lives" is to say that what dies is reborn in some way, resurrected, brought back. There is a sun on the horizon in the Death card, and though it may be tempting to assume it's a sunset, you will notice its location in the east. It's rising.

Joseph Campbell said that the mythic hero's journey contained three distinct phases: departure, initiation, and return. The departure stage begins with a hero who is not yet a hero receiving a "call to adventure." The could-be hero often refuses the call at first (not at all unlike the denial that happens in the precontemplation stage of change). But when they do decide to heed their summoning, they're often met by a benevolent, supportive aide who nudges them along and offers some sort of charm for the road: an object with magical powers, an incantation, a protective talisman. After departure comes the initiation stage, which has to do with the mystery of death in tarot, and it is during this stage that the hero often enters a seemingly inescapable situation, or as Campbell calls this phase "the belly of the whale."

The obvious reference here is to the biblical tale of Jonah, in which God tells a young man to travel to the city of Nineveh to preach to the residents and warn them of God's coming judgment. When Jonah chooses to refuse the call and flee the mission, he is punished; once aboard a boat to a different city, a massive storm arises, threatening everyone on board. When the sailors realize that the storm is in fact the result of Jonah's disobedience to God, he is tossed overboard and swallowed by a whale.

Still alive inside the whale's stomach, Jonah prays and asks forgiveness for three days and three nights. Finally, God demands that the enormous fish vomit up the young man—some say a foreshadowing of Jesus's death and resurrection. To the outside world, a man appears to have perished, but in actuality he has not. And this reveals the mysteries of the life-death-life cycle: having died, a person, place, or thing is inevitably reborn again, and in that process, it is transformed.

Those who know old stories and the arc of the hero's journey understand that rebirth is not to be taken as a promise of ease. Actually, the hero's close encounter with death and reemergence is only the initiation onto a greater path, it sets in motion a whole new set of trials that the hero must then face before beginning the return home. I say this not to scare those going through a death of some kind, or to make you lose heart, but simply to ensure that you will be prepared for what lies ahead. It's easy to want to gloss over the less palatable aspects of death and say, "Transformation is good! You want this, trust me!" But we're not talking renewal and rejuvenation here. This isn't about a day at the spa.

Philosopher Ananda Coomaraswamy wrote that "no creature can attain a higher grade of nature without ceasing to exist," stern words about the reality of growth and transformation. In the language of psychology, it is not so much the self that must cease to exist, but everything that is not the self—the defense mechanisms, maladaptive conditionings, destructive coping strategies, the behaviors that developed in response to childhood trauma that paradoxically seem to invite more trauma in adulthood. These are the things that must die in order for us to transform.

Campbell said of death, "You don't understand death, you learn to acquiesce in death." The Hanged Man met us on the path and pressed charms into our palms to aid us in surrender and acceptance, but that doesn't make it easy. Just as Jonah and countless heroes in old tales have been chucked overboard against their wishes, it's a rare character that goes whistling, willingly into initiation.

A sign that you're being brought into a new form or phase is that you feel hopelessly boxed in like Jonah did with the whale, you haven't seen the sun in days, and the old charms you had seem to have lost their powers overnight. It's uncomfortable. And when the parts of us that are sturdy enough to endure the fire of transformation make it through to what's on the other side, as sure as the sun will rise, there will be a whole new set of learning to do.

Temperance

he ways that seeing the world in pairs of opposites—as either good or bad, black or white, this or that —affects our lives are endless. Systemic oppression is made possible by creating rigid categories of people and then maintaining the illusion that such divisions are legitimate. Racism, sexism, homophobia, ableism, and all the ways we create social in- and out-groups are probably an outward expression of the ways in which we do this in our interior lives, employing extreme, catastrophic, or black-and-white thinking to make sense of the world within and around us.

Because this way of thinking has been correlated with anxiety and depression, it's often a target in counseling. For instance, a person who can see things only in terms of extreme opposites might feel depressed and believe in that moment that suffering is all life ever is, even if just last week they were feeling connected, creative, and alive. That all-or-nothing vision colors the way they act in those moments, the choices they make, and creates problems for them. So the work might then be learning to temper extremes in thinking that lead to unnecessary suffering.

Therapy models like dialectical behavior therapy (DBT) teach people to challenge this natural tendency of the human mind and to think in a way that can synthesize opposites rather than exacerbate stark divisions. When we learn to accommodate the reality that what our brains tend to categorize as opposites can actually both be true at once, we can make more informed and well-rounded decisions. For example, we can acknowledge that we're doing our best while also knowing that we need to do better. We can accept that skillful people sometimes make mistakes and that good people can behave in hurtful ways. Too often, when we view things as cut-and-dried, we discount important information that could help us make better choices for ourselves and those around us.

Much of the tendency to sort and label things as either good or bad is just our brains doing what they've evolved to do. Ancient humans who were able to quickly discern something safe from something dangerous were the ones who survived, while those who weren't, did not. That trait was passed down over time, and here we are, sorting and labeling our days away. And there are countless examples of the way that the ability to do this is still useful for our growth and evolution.

On top of being predisposed to categorizing all things into pairs of opposites, when we experience trauma the sorting can become amplified. To protect ourselves from getting hurt again, and because the nuance and ambiguity of life leaves too much to chance, the brain creates rigid categories: all good and all bad. But this makes it hard, if not impossible, to navigate long-term relationships and endeavors because nothing in this world is only beautiful or only flawed. It becomes hard to make decisions because no choice is perfect, and it makes it tough to stick with things that contain high and low moments, as things tend to do. In many ways, healing from trauma is learning to hold polarities, to be in life's gray areas again. It is also the path of the mystic, who wishes to experience the truth and *totality of things*: the good, the bad, and the ugly at once.

Tarotist Rachel Pollack has written that at the root of our dualistic thinking is a fear that we don't know ourselves. We see things as either *this* or *that* because we don't trust ourselves to flexibly navigate the contingencies and the in-betweens and the constant flux that is life and to still be okay. The poet Wolfram von Eschenbach, author of one of the most well-known versions of the Grail legend, *Parzival*, wrote that the Grail—a sacred treasure—was left behind on earth, guarded by angels. Not just any angels, but the ones who remained neutral during the feud between God and Satan, the ones who held the middle ground. The angel in the Temperance card—who stands with one foot on land and one in water—gives us the secret that with practice we, too, can learn to plant our feet in two worlds. We can take what we glean from both this and that and integrate them without slipping. When we can do this, we start on a journey not only to psychological growth but also to spiritual evolution, where we can eventually come into communion with the way things really are.

A secret of Temperance is that there is more than one truth to every situation, that it is possible to hold paradox. That because our brains have evolved in favor of limited perspectives, if we hope to see reality, we must actively seek alternative viewpoints to thicken our narratives whenever possible. We should notice where we've assumed that life should be all pleasant or all painful, where we cannot make space for imperfection, and where to be right, or even just okay, we might have to make another wrong. We should remember that all of this is our nature, and there's room to grow.

The Devil

olk interpretations of the Devil describe an experience of oppression that is, at least in some part, internal rather than exclusively imposed by an outside force. This reading derives from the illustration, which shows that the chains around the necks of the captives are loose enough that they could lift them off themselves should they choose to, which hints at the possibility that their stuckness is a choice. In psychological terms, this might be called learned helplessness.

Choice is an interesting concept because it implies consciousness and capacity to do something different. I think about the Devil a lot in the context of addictive behaviors, which tend to happen compulsively and with a degree of exertion from an unconscious will. There is so little space between stimulus and response that the behavior feels automatic. This is probably one of the reasons why mindfulness-based therapies seem to be effective in the treatment of addictive behaviors. By cultivating a bit of distance between the thinker and the thoughts (or the feeler and the feelings) through the practice of observing internal events as they unfold, a space is created where a person can choose to do something different in response to distressing material, rather than always reaching for the habitual reaction that ultimately breeds more suffering.

What's often overlooked about addictive behavior is that, when the primary goal is to manage pain—whether it be psychological, physical, or a combination of the two (as is so often the case)—things like alcohol or painkillers or sex or slot machines or shopping or exercising are actually really effective. This isn't to reduce addiction to simple avoidance; it's a complex process—often with biological, social, ecological, and psychological components—that's rarely as simple as using behaviors to avoid thoughts and feelings you don't want. But if the primary goal is to keep thoughts, feelings, and sensations under control and at a level that you can live with, engaging in a behavior that suppresses, masks, or numbs is a genius strategy. You're not "crazy" for doing that, you're smart.

Obviously a lot of addictive behaviors aren't sustainable in the long term, and the habitual use of these behaviors typically comes at a pretty high cost. But these are coping strategies, so while they may do nothing to support your evolution, they work when you've got nothing else to choose from.

And by the way, if no one around you had better methods or taught you any effective ways to manage what scares you, I'd say you deserve a ton of grace and compassion for finding what's worked and sticking with it. I'm not going to go so far as to pat you on the back for it, but I certainly don't blame you.

Another thing that I think is crucial to know about addictive behavior is that when we avoid something, we experience temporary peace or relief from the thorniness of that thing. This reinforces the avoidant behavior, but it also reinforces the belief that the thing we're avoiding is dangerous. Peter Levine, who has written and taught extensively on somatic approaches to healing trauma, writes that "whatever experiences you turn away from, the brain-body registers as dangerous." A lot of times the things we're avoiding are feelings, such as grief or anxiety. And so in avoiding grief or anxiety, we're also investing in this broader belief that feelings themselves have the capacity to be dangerous—and that's just not true.

Psychologist Delia Kostner has written that "it is the elaborate ways in which we turn away from pain through psychological defenses that leads to the increase and elaboration of pain." It seems to me that this belief—that certain thoughts, feelings, or sensations are themselves dangerous—is one of the things with the most power to undermine a vital life and create patterns that exacerbate and maintain suffering.

We slip a chain around our own necks every time we make certain thoughts, feelings, or sensations bigger and more powerful than they actually are. When we believe grief or loneliness or fears of social rejection are dangerous in and of themselves, and then fashion whole lives around avoiding them. We think we're free of the feeling when in truth we're enslaved by it. Chained to and cursed to haul its weight around for eternity, or until we're ready to engage with it in a way that isn't about dominance or suppression or control. There is nothing maladaptive about wanting to avoid what is frightening or unpleasant. Just make sure that what you're scared of is actually dangerous before you go building a whole life around avoiding it.

The Tower

Psychiatrist Harry Stack Sullivan believed that the core motivating force for all human behavior is anxiety, and that our personalities are essentially a collection of habits and strategies we gather over time to minimize anxiety, avoid disapproval, and preserve a positive sense of self. Though the development of a personality is obviously much more complex than that, the Tower can be understood as symbolizing the particular personality traits that function as a sort of buffer against the anxiety of living. And from this perspective, the Tower can go from being one of the most feared cards in the deck to a powerful blessing.

In old stories, the Divine sometimes appears as a creator and sometimes as a destroyer. But even if we're intellectually able to understand the falling of the Tower as a function of some divine force that builds and tears down for eternity, somehow that doesn't make it any less terrifying. When our towers crumble, we're thrust headfirst into a direct experience of the stuff that's struck terror in our hearts since infancy and that we've been unconsciously avoiding ever since. If our personality, our tower, is built with the bricks of behavioral patterns that make us feel protected from what we perceive as threatening, including the experience of anxiety itself, when we begin to pluck those bricks out, we feel vulnerable and exposed. Exposed to the elements of social rejection, abandonment, unworthiness, failure, unlovability, and isolation.

One core belief that I think forms the foundation of many towers is that anxiety itself is dangerous and must be avoided at all costs. This isn't a ridiculous thing to believe, given that when we're young and dependent on the adults in our lives, our biggest anxiety is rooted in abandonment by our caregivers. Rejection would be tantamount to death. So as we grow, we learn to behave in ways that will minimize our greatest anxiety: the fear of being rejected and ultimately abandoned. This fear of rejection and, in turn, of death is completely human. But as we age we can grow into the reality that the source of our most deep-rooted anxiety—interpersonal abandonment—will not kill us.

The Tower falls when we realize that anxiety in itself is not dangerous. The danger comes from the intricate ways we attempt to outrun and escape it. These patterns of avoidance are what create problems for us beyond the natural pain of living. But there are simply better and more life-giving ways to cope with stress than building patterns that act like cement walls. When we come to understand that yes, our psychological defense structures have served a protective function, but no, we don't actually need that particular kind of armor to survive, a new life becomes possible.

We built walls in a time when we thought that anxiety itself was a threat to life, but the reality is we can both tolerate and learn from it. We can live with not being liked, we can survive being misunderstood, we can make mistakes, we can feel bad. Having released the goal of avoiding discomfort as much as humanly possible and by any and all means necessary, we free ourselves up to pursue new visions that aren't about the absence of suffering but rather the pursuit of fulfillment, connection, and the stuff that makes life worth living. What a relief this turns out to be. To realize that not only can we take our walls down, we can do so regardless of whether anxiety goes away. We can live really beautiful, fulfilling lives *with* anxiety instead of feeling like we have to avoid it.

The Star

What makes having hope so hard for some people and not for others? Can you nurture hope where it's already living or revive it where it seems to have shrunk back or dried up altogether? Through the years I've noticed that the practice of hope is one thing to profess, and yet another to practice.

The question of what makes hoping harder for some than others is an important one. Given our complex histories, so much of which we had no choice or say in, it is unconscionable that any person should feel as though their difficulty maintaining hope has to do with a personal defect or shortcoming. Not all people have the conditioning and temperament to imagine the future as one that's likely to be favorable, or even safe.

Hopelessness is a core feature of depression, for example, and to take that deeper, I'd argue it's also a feature of being a person who was never afforded the luxury of feeling safe early in life. It is not at all wrong for a person with a track record of not having their needs met to have a hard time believing that, one day, they will. Why take the emotional risk of believing in something that has literally no evidence of being realistic or practical? In a very real sense, a lack of hope can be seen as adaptive, protective, and wise. In severe cases, a lack of hope can keep us alive in an environment where to suffer one more blow of deep disappointment could be the thing that does us in.

Psychologist Erik Erikson believed that in each stage of our development we experience a crisis that—should all go according to an ideal plan for human living—allows us to emerge on the other side with a virtue. The very first crisis, which he believed occurred from birth to age two, is when an infant negotiates between trust and mistrust. This is when infants determine whether or not they can trust in the world and the people in it. Depending on what they experience at this point, either they emerge with the virtue of hope, or they develop qualities like suspicion, mistrust, and anxiety. You can imagine, then, what you might emerge with if you were surrounded by people who were inconsistent in their ability to respond to you as a baby. Hope is something we either learn or don't learn very early, and it's easy to see how that might color our lives from then on.

The Star is often interpreted as a harbinger of hope. But without a willingness to examine the barriers to hope—to a genuine belief in things working out—I often fear that its medicine could be insoluble, that the message will fall flat. At the very least, perhaps the Star can be an invitation to all those having a hard time with hope to give themselves grace around why that is.

Grace in practice looks like reminding yourself that it isn't your fault if hope feels hard, and that odd as it may sound, hopelessness may have actually been the thing that protected you all these years. Something you did because you loved yourself so much you weren't willing to put yourself through one more disappointment. Because you had the inborn wisdom to know that to wish even once more in a circumstance that couldn't and wouldn't change might have shattered you. I'm not sure what Erikson would have said about this, and certainly my own privilege factors into the capacity to hold this view and really believe it, but I think it's never too late to go back and claim our lost virtues: will, purpose, love, wisdom, and hope.

The Moon

n a culture that worships at the altar of knowledge, confusion is generally seen as void of value. Disorientation is pathologized and understood as a condition to be remedied and rid of as quickly as possible. A reflection of this collective bias toward knowing, people who seek counsel through tarot tend to fear the Moon because it appears to be the opposite of what they think they need: clarity, guidance, answers.

When trying to understand a dream, one of the first things you do is identify your associations with the settings and symbols in the dream. What does a moon mean to you? The moon has to do with nighttime. What is nighttime? It is a time when what we see clearly during the day is obscured and cast in shadow. Do you ever notice how anxiety tends to get worse at night? Like children terrorized by their own visions of monsters under the bed, we project our fears into the spaces and times when we cannot see what's there. You may be wondering, as I have, what use a symbol of confusion could possibly have to those feeling lost or stuck.

One evening over tapas and grenache, a friend and mentor from graduate school told me about a technique that therapists use to stimulate confusion in clients by relating to them in a way they're not expecting or asking a question that challenges their default logic or mode of thinking. It may sound odd—perhaps even cruel or unusual—to intentionally confuse another person, especially one you're supposed to be helping, but bear with me. When someone who's been stuck gets confused, the tight path they've been walking vanishes and they're forced to forge a new way.

Part of the work in tarot is learning to open ourselves up to the spectrum of life experiences, learning to dwell between the night and day, unconscious and conscious, forest and village. The idea that confusion could have therapeutic value is powerful because it takes a human condition that's generally thought to be negative and suggests that it could actually be a kind of crucible. It probes into the possibility that confusion could actually be an ideal time for working on our ancient and atrophied modes of seeing, moving, and knowing. It marvels and wonders aloud: If I could be with mystery just a while longer without needing to make it go away, could a new way of navigating emerge? Is it within the realm of possibility that stepping out from the ice house of conscious knowing might actually make way for something more low to the ground, more instinctual, or from a higher state of consciousness? Is it possible that confused times are actually perfect openings to call on parts of ourselves that we can't otherwise access?

After that dinner I couldn't resist doing more research into the healing properties of confusion. As it turns out, healers and teachers have been using confusion as a tool since time out of mind. Zen koans— ancient riddles used by Zen Buddhists in meditation—date back centuries and are designed to help people better understand the nature of reality by puzzling them and in doing so revealing the limitations of knowing with the analytic mind. As one particularly well-known koan goes: "When both hands are clapped a sound is produced; listen to the sound of one hand clapping." A classroom study was widely publicized after researchers found that when teachers stimulated states of confusion in their students, the students learned more. And in the field of mental health, psychiatrist Milton Erickson taught "confusion techniques" to hypnotherapists, who learned to use disorientation in therapy to help patients change.

To know something for certain is the psychic equivalent of building a wall against anything that could challenge that knowledge. For instance, if I assume certain feelings—like anger, fear, or sadness—are dangerous, that assumption is a wall that's going to keep me from doing anything that might trigger those feelings whether I'm conscious of it or not. Someone who thinks they know for certain that they're terrible at algebra might really want to be an economist but, without even questioning it, avoids any course of study that requires mathematics. How many people with the potential to change the world don't do so because of what they believe they know for sure about their capabilities and shortcomings?

As holding paradox remains the continual lesson of tarot, knowledge is beautiful and we seek it even as we understand the ways in which knowing things is limiting. Knowing can expand what we see as possible, but it can also be like a box we settle into where we unconsciously defend against our own growth. To be in a state of not knowing creates openings, illuminates new pathways, and is thus ripe with potential, even as what we can't grasp yet may scare us. When defenses drop, new edges and footholds appear, and when we're flailing, we're a lot less picky about what we grab hold of to stay alive.

The Sun

There's a very old and popular fairy tale about a frog and a young princess. The two become friends after the young princess's beloved golden ball flies down a dark well and the frog, good with plunging depths and more comfortable than she is in damp dark spaces, offers to retrieve it in exchange for companionship. The golden ball is a common symbol of the self in old stories, whose function is, according to Jungian analyst Marie-Louise von Franz, "to unite the dark and light aspects of the psyche."

A frog who dwells at the bottom of musty wells and a princess who sleeps high in a castle at night come together and what happens is not unlike what happens when we start to unearth the hidden mysteries in our psychology. I'll spare the details here but suffice it to say that when the frog insists on eating from the princess's plate and sleeping on her pillow, there's aggravation, irritation, and disgust. You may know the feeling. It's not unlike trying to have a nice meal or fall asleep at night after someone's just told you that you did something manipulative, or when you've suddenly realized you'd been doing the absolute most just to avoid looking down into some deep well of grief.

How is it exactly that parts of us become frogs and get cast down into these wells in the first place? For starters, each and every one of us has been experiencing rejection from the moment we were born. And while it may sound Brothers Grimm–level dramatic, it's fact, not fairy tale. Our personalities developed in part based on the cues we were given from infancy by our caregivers about what is and isn't acceptable. We came into this world sorting what's okay about us and what isn't. *This*—smiling, obedience, agreeability—*this* gets to live up in the big fluffy bedroom on the third floor of the castle. *That*—dissent, rapacious desire, the urge to control everything and everyone—*that's* stuff for the depths, cast it down into the well way out by the property line.

Our parents or caregivers had preferences before we were born and those preferences didn't go away when we arrived in this world. They had visions and fantasies about what it meant to be a parent or to have a child. Those ideas were placed firmly upon us and, not because they were bad people but because they were human, our caregivers chose our names before we were even born. Before we had a chance to show the world what our eyes look like when we're happy, what it feels like to be in a room with us when we're scared, or how we can sometimes hear colors. Far more than we were ever invited to be who we truly are, we were told who we should be.

Poet and storyteller Robert Bly wrote, "The drama is this. We came as infants, 'trailing clouds of glory,' arriving from the farthest reaches of the universe.... In short with our 360 degree radiance.... And we offered this gift to our parents. They didn't want it. They wanted a nice girl or a nice boy. That's the first act of the drama."

Each and every one of us experienced this rejection of who we truly are and came here to be in some form. Because someone was counting on us to be something else, something they needed us to be, a supporting role in their own story. This old rejection wound is like a beast we lug around. It sometimes sleeps, but wakes easily, ready to emerge at the slightest hint of disapproval. Psychologist Alice Miller wrote that even though we betrayed ourselves as children, though we sold out parts of ourselves and threw them down into the deep well, we can't blame ourselves for doing all we really could in the circumstances to survive. The best thing we can do, she writes, is to mourn. But I think there's more.

The symbol of the golden ball as the force that seeks to unite the conscious and unconscious parts of our experience is a drive that is alive and well in you, and I know that because you wouldn't be reading this book if it weren't. Without that drive you'd probably have little interest in cupping your ear to listen for the secrets of something like tarot. You're here because you want to know the truth. And me, too. In the illustration of the Sun, a baby rides a white horse naked through a field of sunflowers with the golden ball, the sun itself, at their backs. The task here is to shine a light on, and in doing so come into relationship with, the creatures that we long ago relegated to the bottoms of the damp wells on the edges of our awareness. It is to courageously follow the bouncing ball into the shadowy forests and see what's there.

In some versions of the frog prince story, the princess gets so frustrated with the frog that she throws him against a wall, while in others, they kiss. But in all versions I've heard, the story ends when the frog magically transforms into a prince, at which point he's finally able to join the princess in a kind of harmonious communion. Just as we each hope to do when we create awareness around our old wounds and patterns so that we might begin to integrate those things as a route toward truer versions of ourselves.

Judgment

aving spent a good amount of time exploring the benefits of things like mindfulness and cognitive therapy, I remain unconvinced that it's possible to choose *not* to think about something. For example, if I sit across from you and tell you not to think about a turquoise rabbit, you'll probably start thinking about a turquoise rabbit. But if you've practiced directing your attention through meditation or training the mind in some other way that works for you, you will likely be more capable of redirecting your focus to something you'd prefer to be thinking about. And the more skilled you are at that, the better you'll be at holding your gaze on those things or bringing it back when it strays, which it will. If you're someone who has the tendency to obsess, worry, or otherwise get carried away by the incessant fluctuations of the mind, the capacity to do this is life altering.

There are two general ways that I read the Judgment card in tarot: as a *call to adventure* and as *resurrection*. A call to adventure is an invitation to change; that is, to leave behind an old way for a new one, to forget who we are *not* and remember who we *are*. Old stories remind us that hearing the call is not the same as answering; many heroes have refused a call at first, sometimes multiple times, just as many of us have declined opportunities to grow until we're ready. Answering the call requires a very specific psychological task, which is that we forget anything that isn't useful to the journey and remember everything that is. And this is where that mindfulness training comes in, and it's also where we start to work with the metaphor of resurrection, an image that we see in many classic illustrations of the twentieth major arcana.

Theologian Richard Bulzacchelli has written that "with resurrection as a metaphor, we choose to live as if life has an eternal and objective meaning, even though we know, at a rational level, that everything must end. It means choosing to put the past behind us and live toward a new future in which the mistakes and losses of the past could be replaced by better choices and new opportunities." In other words, the theme of resurrection is about letting go of or forgetting what will weigh us down on the path forward, in order to make space for the things that we do need, like clarity, lightness, and agility. In fact, many an old-tale hero has also been seen scattering personal items, often of great value (see the character walking away from the eight gilded items in the Eight of Cups on page 209) in order to flee a dangerous situation or attempt to make their way back home after attaining a treasure.

Bulzacchelli wrote that the resurrection story in Christianity, in which the whole body of Jesus Christ is risen rather than the soul only, instructs that "what we're really after is a meaning that endures beyond the boundaries of death, even beyond the boundaries of time and history." The metaphor of resurrection is an affirmation that life has meaning and value that is eternal, not subject to the same withering away imposed on all in the domain of space and time. In less weighty tales, like that of Granadina, the Sardinian version of the Grimms' Snow White, we see a similar motif: a young woman dies after her stepmother poisons her with golden shoes but comes alive again through the love of a prince and his benevolent queen mother.

Both the Christian story of Jesus and the Mediterranean island tale want to pull our attention toward something in us that endures even when subjected to the degenerative and poisonous forces of this world. In resurrection, remembering, or a coming back to life, we also have to forget something: we have to forget about the limitations that come with being human in this physical world. In the age of social media—when we are inundated with traumatic material at a rate unlike any other time in human history—our task is to find a way to continue living in alignment with what's precious even as the world burns around us.

Judgment, carrying both the metaphors of a call to adventure and resurrection, asks: How do we continue to live life in accordance with what we hold to be right and true, even as the world crumbles around us? How do we stay doing what's right, even when it sometimes seems that right is futile in the face of forces of exploitation and destruction that appear to be larger-than-life?

The secret told by Judgment is that we must stay connected to the meaning "that endures beyond the boundaries of death… time and history." That we forget what Joseph Campbell called "the inhuman claims placed upon us" by the systems under which we live and remember that our life has meaning, even if that meaning must stay at least somewhat a mystery. That we remember *every* life has meaning.

Every cry for climate justice, racial justice, and all other forms of social justice is a call to adventure, and each day we stand at the crossroads—depicted by the symbol of the cross in the flag of the Judgment angel—given the option to refuse the call or answer it. What we need to do in order to choose the latter is to forget all that isn't useful to that journey and remember all that is. The limitations of being alive in a human body with finite levels of attention and capacities for empathy mean that we do have to consciously forget certain things in order to function. But in order to continuously move forward, we have to remember the deep care for one another that makes us human, what constitutes the right thing, and a sense of belonging to something greater than the isolated flesh house of the self.

The World

hysicist David Bohm, who dedicated his life to understanding the nature of reality, wrote that it is "vast, rich, and in a state of unending flux of enfoldment and unfoldment, with laws most of which are only vaguely known, and which may even be ultimately unknowable in their totality." He asserted that, ultimately, reality as it *truly* is can never be grasped.

One understanding of the World, the twenty-first arcana in tarot, is that it symbolizes an experience of absolute reality. In the words of the mythic Hermes Trismegistus, absolute reality is "all times and places, all substances and qualities and magnitudes together." In a perhaps more practical sense, absolute reality has to do with plurality and inclusivity. It is about the goal of experiencing life as it is, in all its beauty and terror, ambiguity and contradiction.

The personification of these ideas appears in the mythological Mercurius, who was known by the alchemists as a spirit of truth. If you've ever been called "mercurial" it may mean you're prone to unpredictable or erratic shifts—a trait most of us don't love in people we're close to—but in his book *Alchemical Studies*, Carl Jung quotes a text that described Mercurius as "the spirit of the world become body within the earth." This language echoes the concept of an interconnected anima mundi, or dynamic, fluctuating, and complex world soul. Another way of understanding absolute reality.

In modern behavioral therapies, absolute reality is accessed through what psychologist Marsha Linehan describes as the "synthesis of opposites," a way of accommodating two or more seemingly conflicted truths. In dialectical behavior therapy, the therapist's job is to help the client hold both the need for change and the need for radical self-acceptance at once. Both are real, and both are crucial to the process.

I'm connecting dots between ancient and contemporary theories to show continuity in the way we've understood reality across space and time, but the goal isn't to claim that there is one enduring truth, one absolute reality. Psychiatrist Frantz Fanon, a pioneer in liberation psychology, critiqued European psychology for, among other things, its notion of a universal collective unconscious that neglected to address shared "complexes" in the unconscious—hidden thoughts or feelings that were shared but unique to a community or culture. Fanon felt that it was inappropriate to paint broad strokes over diverse experiences. Instead, we should practice curiosity about difference. We should attend to what's actually there. Generalizations and broad strokes are, in that sense, the antithesis of the World. In the words of storyteller Daniel Deardorff, "If we are wise we are inclusive. Wisdom takes advantage of multiple perspectives and intelligences. Wisdom is never one-sided."

Marginalization is a side effect of having a standard or structure that is defined largely by what it is not. Psychologically, such structures are the often one-dimensional personal narratives we carry about who we are (and are not) and what we do (and don't do), stories that cast anything that doesn't fit in with the plotline out past the boundaries of what we're willing to acknowledge as true, or even possible. Unsurprisingly, that same process is replicated in demographic structures that delineate in-groups and out-groups, each depending on the other to tell them who they are by providing an example of who they are not. Mythologist Martin Shaw has written, "The traditional technique when we wish to make an enemy of 'Otherness,' is to reduce it, lessen it, make it ridiculous. If it all possible we will attempt to concrete our wall of defense with race, class, and gender. We reject connection—we may not know who we are but we know we're not *that*."

But Lewis Hyde has written that whatever is excluded from the dominant order always "turns out to be needed in a later time or place."

And so the aim of the World is not to identify sameness but to know the value of both *this* and *that* at once. It is plurality, diversity, space made for all. And it's not fixed but ongoing, a process of both exile and return. Of erecting structures whose nature is to exclude and retrieving and restoring what's been driven past the edges.

The Fool's journey to the World is about *not* choosing between the edge or the center, civilization or the wild, male or female, above or below. Rather, it has more to do with a sacred liminality. Something mercurial, dialectical, absolute. I think tarot itself is a living example of this energy. Like Prometheus stealing fire from the realm of the gods as a gift to the earthbound, the cards also move fluidly between worlds and guide us to do the same. Like all mythological tricksters—Loki, Coyote, Hermes, to name a few—the cards spring like the dancer with one foot on the ground and one in the ether, dropping jewels from the ancients in unexpected places, from behavioral health clinics to community tarot circles, birthday parties and personal rituals. The aim is all of it; it is walking between worlds with as much grace as is possible.

The Minor Arcana

Ace of Wands

any of the therapies that have been and will be discussed in this book are behavioral therapies, which focus on the domain of behavior and the ways in which thoughts and feelings interact to inform behavior and vice versa. One of the reasons that I find tarot to be so powerful is that each card, particularly in the minor arcana, speaks directly to the four domains of human experience and helps us understand how to achieve a level of understanding and competence in each. To understand each of the domains, the ace, which represents the "one" and thus the raw material of that suit, is a helpful starting place.

The swords help us understand cognition, the cups teach us about emotion, and the pentacles whisper secrets about how to use values-aligned behavior to influence how we think and feel. But tarot also includes a fourth domain that's too often overlooked in behavioral therapies: the domain of energy, represented by the wands suit. With the understandable emphasis on evidence-based practice in the mental health field, this domain is often neglected because it's the part of our being that can't be measured.

The wands unite the ethereal with the corporeal. This is symbolized by the fact that they are often seen resting with one end on the ground and one in the air. Its roots are both spiritual and material, one pole in earth and the other in the heavens. In alchemy, the wand would likely be associated with sulfur, the spiritual material that represents the soul and which is seen as the intermediary connecting the mind and body. Modern neuroscience mirrors this alchemical idea;

the image of the wand hints a bit at the human vagus nerve, which connects the brain and gastrointestinal tract, communicates data about different organs to the brain, and is often targeted in "mind-body" approaches to treating mental and physical health concerns.

The wand is traditionally associated with the fire element, warmth being the thing that distinguishes the living from the dead. Fire is a necessary part of any therapeutic process. Even if we're using terms like *hot cognitions* and *dysregulation* to talk about it, we're talking about an energy that has the potential to bring transformation to a person's life. People go to therapy because some fiery energy—something too hot to handle—is fueling maladaptive behaviors or ravaging interpersonal relationships with no sign of slowing down. Often it takes a wildfire of some sort in our lives for us to realize it's time to heal. In religious doctrine, the theme of heat is used to describe an active engagement of faith, as is the case in the New Testament book of Revelation when Jesus says, "Because thou art lukewarm, and neither cold nor hot, I will spew thee out of my mouth."

Though many folk interpretations associate the wands with action, I believe they represent the stuff that precedes action. The wands contain the energy that drives, motivates, and stimulates us. In many decks, wands are called staffs. Jungian analyst Marie-Louise von Franz wrote that "the staff is also associated with the Way and is a direction-giving principle in the unconscious. The bishop's staff, for instance, was interpreted by the church as the authority of the doctrine, which shows the way and gives decisions. In antiquity, the golden staff or magic rod belonged to Mercurius and represents his ability to marshal intractable elements within the unconscious. If one has a staff, one is not wholly passive; one has a direction."

Therefore, I see the wand as having to do with our desires as well as our "intuitive appraisals"—that initial spark of response within us before we have time to think about what something means, and in doing so repress our feelings about that thing or engage in some act of avoidance. Though this stuff is many times shrouded in dry, unmagical language, it is often what clinicians are working toward in a therapy room. The hot stuff, raw stuff, the stuff with the fire in it. Where the potential for new life and new learning lives. It is the more subtle and less measurable material of the human experience that can and does rule the dense, and when we learn to work with it in service of our growth and evolution, that's magic. And that's what the wand does best.

Two of Wands

e often stay stuck for too long in the wrong situations because we don't know how to cope with the disappointment of something not living up to a fantasy we had. When the only way you know how to deal with disappointment is to avoid it, you're at especially high risk of getting stuck, because life is full of things not being what we thought they would be. It's important to our evolution that we learn to live with that.

It can feel like a cruel joke to get a taste of something you've spent years longing for, only to realize that it's not what you want at all. I recall countless times in life having the distinct experience of recognizing, "Oh, wow, this isn't what I thought it was," but being unwilling or unable to sit with the disappointment that came with accepting that. Not knowing how to walk away from the fantasy I'd constructed, uncertain how to carry the grief, the loneliness, the fear of it never being better, the very particular dread of deprivation, I'd stay with a thing—a job, a relationship, a living space—knowing in the lining of my stomach and the valves of my heart that it wasn't what I wanted. Looking back, more often than not, it wasn't even close.

The Two of Wands shows a person in a high tower wearing fancy clothes overlooking a beautiful vista, yet gazing off into the distance, yearning for something else. In Pamela Colman Smith's version of this card, the person is wearing a red cap on their head, suggesting that passion and life are alive and well but confined to the idea space. The rest of the body is draped in muted tones, which stands for the reality of day-to-day life, which has taken on the color of a barren field as the figure isn't in the right space to grow. It isn't that the fantastic views and expensive clothes aren't nice or pleasurable, it's just that they aren't what this person deeply needs. If you've ever experienced this kind of scenario yourself, you know how it goes. It starts out as discomfort: the clothing doesn't fit right, you're always tugging at it and adjusting, you feel awkward about it in public. As time goes on, it starts to actually hurt. The too-snug waistband is cinching your organs; the turtleneck makes it hard to breathe.

I've often seen this card as representing a call to adventure, like the young Siddhārtha Gautama, the Buddha, living as a privileged prince in a palace but longing for more. His story resonates with so many of all faiths and creeds because it tells of the rewards in store for those with the courage to follow the heart's longings, even when they're drastically out of step with what our societies teach us to want. Perhaps especially then. Siddhārtha renounced his worldly status and belongings, later found enlightenment, and has gained eternal life in the hearts and minds of human beings ever since. If that's not a teaching to go for what one requires, I don't know what is. But the Buddha's path was not easy; he had to first be willing to face how disappointed he was with his existing life circumstances. He had to accept that what was enough for others was not enough for him. It was that acceptance that allowed him to move forward.

The human mind has this ability to construct elaborate fantasies that are so powerful that when reality doesn't match up, we're often perplexed, completely unaware of what's happened. People go years trapped inside the dissonance between what they'd hoped for and what is. But there is another option. We always have the choice either to stay trapped in that tight space between the thing we wanted and the thing we got, or to buck up and feel the disappointment that comes with accepting that reality is not what we'd hoped for. We get to essentially choose between two emotional experiences: feeling disappointed or feeling stuck.

Each choice has its side effects. If you choose to feel the disappointment, you might also experience a sense of hopelessness, fear, inadequacy, and the bumping up against prickly core beliefs about the world and its ability to meet your needs. If you choose to feel stuck, you'll probably experience frustration, a sense that your instincts have dulled to the point that you're not sure which way is up, a loss of vitality, and in severe cases, anhedonia (the inability to feel pleasure) and depression. But another thing you should know is that the side effects of disappointment will dissipate as you accept that the choice you made is not what you wanted and move forward from that place. If you choose to feel stuck, the side effects that come with that—the frustration, numbing of the instincts, disorientation—will only grow.

Some of us learn by choosing stuckness until it's no longer bearable. It wasn't the case with Siddhārtha, but many heroes deny the call to adventure at first. You should know that it's 100 percent okay to choose stuckness. Choosing stuckness is your birthright. And don't worry, the disappointment will be there waiting for you when you're good and ready to feel it.

Three of Wands

My friend, therapist Charles Hattman, once told me that a counselor is usually doing one of two things in the therapy room: supporting the client or frustrating them. He told me this over dinner, and I looked at him confused. Supporting, yes, but why on earth would anyone pay to be frustrated when life is so frustrating already, when frustration is likely what brought them to the therapy room in the first place? He went on to clarify that the stuckness—the fear of change that creates the scenarios worthy of therapeutic work—has to be frustrated; it needs to be seen, seized, and held under the light. It has to be challenged and confronted.

Tarot reading is similar. People who seek counsel through the cards are often also either looking for support through affirmation that they're on the right path, or looking to make a big life change and needing to be frustrated in their current mode of thinking or behaving so that they might better understand what's stopping them. When there are a million and one reasons to not do a scary thing, tarot can give counterarguments, good luck charms, and life-giving templates to step into.

The Three of Wands follows the Two of Wands with a sharply contrasting image—between being in the comforts of a cohesive, settled life (Two of Wands) and striking out on one's own, into the haphazard, incoherent wilds of what Joseph Campbell called "the uninterpreted life." Here is an image of the liminal stage of initiation into a mythic hero's quest, the path of someone whose dream doesn't align with the framework they're in or have been given, and who must therefore venture into the "dark forest... of original experience." This is a path toward something that is not yet cohesive, where you must do your own transcribing and arranging, and where, as Campbell said, "you've got to work out your life for yourself."

On quite a regular basis I find myself reminding people that, in Maslow's hierarchy of needs, the—albeit controversial—pyramid of human necessities starts with the most basic physiological requirements like air, food, and shelter, and at the very top are belonging and, ultimately, self-actualization. That means that if the biggest concerns in your life are about feeling dissatisfied, unfulfilled, or creatively stuck, you are actually extremely fortunate. That's not to shame you for your privileges but to remind you that you are safe. Because when we are safe, we are more free to take risks and to be brave with our lives.

So if you do find yourself standing between worlds, wanting to leap but feeling scared to, if your basic needs are met and then some, if you're asking questions about how to willingly break your own heart, or to be a beginner in a way that feels scary, or abandon a thing that would compromise the lifestyle you've come to depend on, well, you are a lucky one. And I think knowing that gives you a good rock to jump from.

And again, I don't say this to invalidate how hard it is. I say it because I know how easy it is to feel like the house always wins and that it's going to be bad for you, when in reality *you* are the one holding the cards and calling the shots. You are the one deciding that you even want to leave the comfort of the village to venture into the dark forest in the first place.

Four of Wands

hether we call ourselves mystics or not, we spend so much of our lives seeking. As philosopher Josiah Royce writes, "Finite as we are, lost though we seem to be in the woods, or in the 'wide air's wildernesses,' in this world of time and of chance, we have still, like the strayed animals or like the migrating birds, our homing instinct.... We seek."

One manifestation of this seeking is the classic "looking for love in all the wrong places," the ugly duckling wandering around asking every animal, "Are you my mother?" and feeling an increasing sense of exile through the process. Many of us have done this and it's a common symptom among those who never really felt seen or understood in a home of origin. This particular kind of seeking may be evidence of Royce's innate longing for home in the human psyche. Even if we have never felt at home, in the marrow of our bones there is a knowing, a sense that home does exist. That it *must*.

There is a wounding that happens when we feel chronically out of place, whether it's being almost certain we were mistaken for someone else in the hospital nursery at birth and sent home with the wrong family or a long history skirting the edges of the playground, never quite speaking the language of our peers. And when that out-of-placeness is our norm, we can begin to mistake that feeling for what home is. Seekers of familiarity by nature, we are often drawn as if magnetically to situations that replicate what we're used to whether it's good for us or not. Whether it is a well-fitted mantle or a cheap knock-off that never quite sits right.

For many of us, it is a significant developmental task to reset our sense of home so that we are drawn to situations that are affirmative and life giving rather than replicators of the sense of exile we came up with. This is a unique journey that looks different for everyone, and as much as I wish I could tell you the way, I cannot. One thing I can say: the reset usually involves attending to the original wound, where you first felt you were outside and unable to get in. There are many options for treating the wound. Here are a couple.

Option A is that you seek to experience belonging among people and situations that want and desire only certain parts of you. They will decide which parts they want, and it will be on you to determine what to do with the rest. This is a good option if the pain of the original wound is too much to bear and you need a quick salve to numb and soothe in the moment. It won't tend the root of the problem, and long-term use is not recommended; it's associated with exacerbation of symptoms over time and, in severe cases, infection—a sense of exile that only gets worse.

Option B is that you choose to be around people who can accept both your offerings and your vulnerabilities. This means that they recognize your autonomy and hold space for you to deviate from their ideas of what is right, and it means that when you say *when*, that means *when*. It means that you are honored in both what you bring to the table and what you do not, cannot, and will not. Unlike option A, long-term use of option B is associated with good self-esteem, a sense of safety, and a thriving creative life. This is a good option for those who have developed the coping skills to manage the loneliness that radiates from the original wound, and who don't need to numb it just to get through the day. Because there is usually a waiting period for this option, it requires patience and the audacity to believe that if you hold out, it will come. How will you know when you've chosen this option? As Clarissa Pinkola Estés has written, "You will recognize it because it makes your life stronger rather than weaker."

The wands always come with a degree of fire, and because there are four, the suggestion is that the stability of belonging creates a grounding from which creative energy can flow with a certain strength and sustainability. It's common and normal for those seeking home to switch back and forth between option A and option B. Just know that whichever option you're currently using, there is no shame in wanting to belong and to be loved.

Five of Wands

One of the ideas that have been most helpful to me in my own healing work is the possibility that we each contain a diverse "internal family" of psychological parts, and that it's when those parts are in conflict that we tend to feel stuck. This concept comes from the Internal Family Systems model of psychotherapy, developed by Richard Schwartz, who wrote, "It is as if we each contain a society of people, each of whom is at a different age and has different interests, talents, and temperaments," and that "once we get beyond our cultural bias toward viewing ourselves as consistent, unitary individuals, the multiplicity paradigm makes immediate intuitive sense."

When conflict exists among our "internal family" members, we tend to try to pick a side and silence all dissenting parts. But since we can't ever get rid of any of the family members (we can and do exile them, but they don't actually go anywhere and that's another story) we tend to wear ourselves out suppressing one part or another, and locking into the belief that we've finally "made up our mind," only to change it days, hours, sometimes even minutes later.

One of my favorite things to do when I read tarot for others is to allow different cards to represent some of the various parts that are in conflict when someone shows up feeling stuck, and then to validate each part's right to exist. Because even though rejecting them, debating with them, or simply acting like they're not there is tempting, I haven't seen many cases where that works too well in the long run. The parts we attempt to silence or reject have a way of coming back louder and more convincing or showing up in unexpected ways that undermine what decisions we have been able to make.

A person who's debating how and when to leave a cushy but unfulfilling job to pursue something that's more personally meaningful would do well to identify each internal stakeholder as a way of moving toward some kind of agreement. The Queen of Pentacles might represent the part of them that has a deep need for security, while the Page of Wands could signify the part that has a deep desire to take risks and explore. Maybe this person grew up poor with a lot of insecurity around their basic needs being met. In other words, their need to feel safe is adaptive and reasonable. But their present reality is that they have gotten themselves to a place where they are safe enough to take some risks and create some new learning, and so the Page of Wands makes sense, too.

There's a curious—even sacred—thing that also happens in plurality, when we stop trying to pick sides and instead aim to see from multiple perspectives and open up to possibilities beyond the either/or framework. We begin to see new ways to respond to the needs and concerns of our internal family members that don't require an all-or-nothing approach. Perhaps the Page of Wands' need for new growth and exploration can be met after work hours, or on the weekends.

What happens when we step back and make space for all of these parts to exist is that we realize we actually don't have to choose one and get rid of another in order to move forward. The five characters in the Five of Wands image are bumping up against each other and not much is getting done, but none are in actual danger, they're just different. Ultimately, it's the part of us that looks over the Five of Wands from a bit of distance that does the decision making, not any one part in the image. When we see the parts there in front of us, as this image invites us to do, we realize on an experiential level that who we truly are is probably not any one of those parts and therefore it is not the task to choose one. We get to be the sky, as Buddhist nun Pema Chödrön says, and realize that "everything else—it's just the weather."

Six of Wands

ealing processes often begin with a reckoning, an acknowledgment of the physical manifestations of the invisible things we carry. Behavior is how we express such things in the material realm; it is our way of speaking aloud otherwise concealed truths. The ways we move can reveal so much about what's underneath the surface of the physical body, but it requires that we do a kind of deep, subterranean listening. The kind of listening that all processes of healing require.

Achieving is a behavior that, because it's one that's rewarded and revered in our culture, is rarely questioned. As is the case with all behaviors, there are causes and there are effects that come with achievement. Depending on the nature of accomplishments, the effects can range from a healthier sense of self, confidence, and improved boundaries to pride in excess, rigidity, and hubris.

Intention is important, of course, but not more so than impact. There are times when our motivations to achieve sprout from deep roots in personal values and a desire to use the gifts we've been given for the greater good. Other times, we achieve with the secret intention of proving that we are good or worthy, once and for all. Success in the former tends to yield satisfaction, fulfillment, and a fortified sense of self. The latter is more likely to drain, frustrate, and diminish. As the saying goes, you can never get enough of what you don't actually need.

What we don't yet know from personal experience we can learn from myths and old stories. Any keeper of stories knows and won't hesitate to tell you that excessive pride foreshadows conflict or punishment. The Greeks told of young Icarus, who was given wings of feathers and wax made by his father, Daedalus the inventor. Intoxicated by the thrill of flight—and who wouldn't be—Icarus flew too close to the sun. As he got closer to the flaming ball of light, his waxen wings melted and he plunged tragically to his death. Dramatic an example as this may be, it gets the point across: having a personal quest in life is important, but an overinflated sense of one's power often comes with dire consequences.

The Six of Wands is often understood as telling secrets about victory. A person on horseback, crowned by laurels, is an image of recognition and of having overcome some hardship. If we understand the sequence of each suit as containing a kind of chronological significance—which we don't have to, but it can certainly offer us clues if we do—it may at first seem strange that, having emerged from the chaos of the Five, a card about victory is followed up by the stressful Seven, uncertain Eight, exhausted Nine, and utterly overwhelmed Ten. If the Six of Wands represents victory, why is it followed by the Ten of Wands, with its image of a person laboring with their face hidden, a signifier of burnout and a diminished sense of self?

Venture capital consultant John R. O'Neill wrote that "every present success can be seen to contain a shadow that can become devastating," which sounds like a bummer, but I think the idea behind it is that sometimes what we view as achievement is simply succeeding in the ways we always longed to succeed as children. We feel good enough, nice enough, smart enough, finally. O'Neill goes on to write that "the ego is only prancing because the shadow is really in control." When we are proud, how often is it because we are truly satisfied by our efforts and how often are we just relieved to be holding the parts of ourselves we see as bad and unworthy under wraps, hidden away and concealed below the surface level of our lives?

The Greek story of Icarus gives us clues into what happens when we don't stop to check in with why we're doing what we're doing, and how the things we're achieving make us feel deep down inside. The winged man flies up and up and up for no discernible reason other than because he can, only to come crashing down. I can't tell you how many people I've worked with who have what appear to be fantastic jobs, beautiful families, and picturesque homes, yet feel chronically threatened (Seven of Wands), uncertain (Eight of Wands), exhausted (Nine of Wands), directionless and utterly diminished (Ten of Wands).

If we find that we always need to be right, become intensely distressed at the slightest hint of criticism, refuse to engage with anything that might be a challenge, or feel hollow inside despite being viewed by others as excessively fortunate or lucky, it may be time to ask questions about how we define success, where that definition came from, and how we might revise it to make it more true.

Seven of Wands

s a graduate student I used to sit in on therapy groups with people who'd been diagnosed with major depressive and bipolar disorders. The therapist who ran these groups, Charles "Charlie" Hattman, a Gemini, was a master in using language and conversation to both support and challenge people.

One of the things Charlie used to say that always stuck with me was that when it comes to anger, "nobody *actually blows up*. That's not a thing. No one melts down." And his point was that we're so afraid of fury—our own and others'—that we've created this stigmatizing and hostile language for it that's really not useful. He went on to show the group how to use mindfulness to notice the physiological cues of anger as a way to learn to be curious about, befriend, and ultimately work with this energy in a more effective way.

Language is symbolic, so rageful "explosions," though perhaps not literally explosive, do happen. And if we can curb the knee-jerk reaction to bury ourselves in shame around these experiences, they can be powerful moments for learning. It can definitely be scary to be on the receiving end of someone else's anger, especially if you grew up in a home with rage-driven abuse. But if you're not in danger, and can learn to regulate yourself while on the receiving end, you can learn a lot about the person you're dealing with by what they say when they're angry. You can learn a lot about yourself by what you say when you're angry, too.

Angry interactions with loved ones can be some of the most painful but can also present us with some of the best opportunities for healing, because it's when we're in what psychologist Aaron Beck called "hot cognitions" that our oldest wounds become visible. If we think about how much of our dysfunctional behavior in adult relationships stems from having not been adequately listened to as children, and then having had to craft elaborate ways of getting our needs met in other, often bizarre ways, it strikes me as extremely important that we learn the art of using intimate relationships to heal.

A great place to start is deep empathic listening. And while it's probably not realistic to expect to do this kind of listening 100 percent of the time, we can all start with doing it when we can tell someone close to us is feeling threatened, afraid, agitated, or angry. As long as you're safe, when someone you love starts to look a little bit like the person on the Seven of Wands—quills out, shaky, ready for a fight—see if you can quiet your own defenses enough that you might drop in and listen. From there, you'll have lots of good stuff to work with.

When practicing empathic listening, notice when you hear statements that include the words *never, always,* or other absolute terms. If you are able, you might reply with a reflection like "I'm hearing that you don't feel heard and that this is something you've felt for a long time. That sounds really painful." This doesn't mean you agree or that you're admitting to doing something to cause this feeling. It means you're cocreating an alternative experience for someone who is most likely expecting to *not* be listened to, perhaps even punished for their feelings. By doing so, you're helping them revise the blueprint of what relationships look and feel like. You're doing something that all healers do, facilitating reparation through relationships.

It's also good to acknowledge that emotions evolve for certain reasons, and anger is no different. Validating fury in ourselves and others isn't simply a means to an end of making it go away—if your goal is to squash it, you're not really validating anything. Evolutionary psychology researchers have suggested a thing called the recalibration theory of anger, which suggests that anger evolved to help us increase our social bargaining power and ensure that we demand better deals for ourselves when we've either been slighted or might be again. So, when we've been wronged in some way, being able to feel and process our anger allows us to procure better treatment for ourselves in the future. And as important as it is to be compassionate, empathetic, understanding, loving, and kind, it is also important and valuable—when necessary—to be angry.

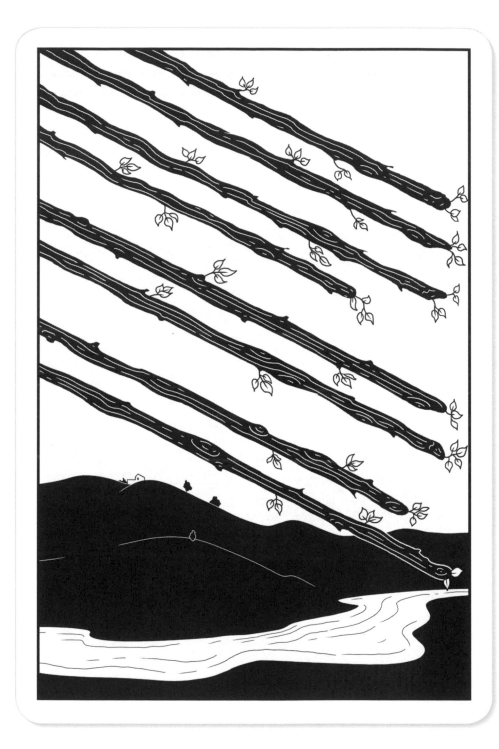

Eight of Wands

 couple of years before writing this book, I was sitting on the edge of an outdoor café with my yoga teacher in Berkeley. I'd been studying Mysore-style Ashtanga yoga with him for several years by then, and I was grateful to be connecting outside of the practice room, thankful to hear his thoughts on things other than postures and energy. I'd left the Bay Area at that point, was living on the East Coast, and was back in Berkeley only for a visit. I was somewhat bashfully telling him that I was unsure leaving had been the right move.

I'd made a big deal about leaving, but, living in the reality of my decision, I was doubting it. When he said something to the effect of "you'll have to wait and see," I remember wishing he would just tell me what I should do. And I'm paraphrasing here, but he didn't do that; instead he said that all of life is a balance of exerting willpower and allowing. That we're always learning which to do when, many times catching ourselves trying to control when we ought to be letting go.

I've thought about those words a lot since then, particularly when I look at the Eight of Wands, which is interpreted by some early tarotists as having to do with swift movement. It's a card that always leaves me with more questions than answers. Where did these wands come from, where are they going, what is this place, where are all the people, what does a raw energy of swiftness mean when there's nothing else attached to it? Swiftly what?

The wands symbolize the subtle stuff of life. Working well with the tacit requires a kind of tuning that is receptive to the less visible aspects of our experience, to the domains of our being that go beyond just the physical. The Eight of Wands, to me, asks questions about what falls within our personal field of energy and what falls beyond it. In more practical terms, this might mean determining what is inside your sphere of influence, and what is not.

Imagine you launch eight wands into the air. Here's what's in your sphere of influence: how much force you used, how much training you did beforehand, what your posture was like, how your breath was, what you were standing on. The rest? That's up to something else. How they land, where they land, what the wind is like that day, how the land slopes, what creature walks by and obstructs the trajectory, and so on. There are secrets in this card about willpower and allowing.

Let's say a friend you really care about doesn't reach out to you as much as you reach out to them. You have a choice here in whether to exert will and say something, or to allow and let it go. Speaking up might be the move; in relationships, communicating your feelings is usually considered a good thing. After sharing what you're going through, you may feel better, and your friend may be glad for the opportunity to adjust their behavior to accommodate you.

The other option is that you consider it your work to accept how your friend shows up—and though this falls more into the allowing category, it's really just a different way of applying will, being *willing* rather than *willful*, as with the former. Rather than exerting will to stimulate your friend changing, you might focus inward, on cultivating the willingness to allow both your friend to be who they are and yourself to have the feelings you do about it. This is allowing, accepting that this is what you've signed up for in a relationship with them.

It's a bit of a pity we can't see the state of the person who's launched these eight wands because I think that would tell us a lot, too. What often makes the allowing part of life so challenging is that when reality doesn't line up with what we want, it's sometimes too painful or uncomfortable to bear. And so we exert will into the world, often on other people, as a way to avoid allowing the truth of what is and how we feel about it.

For instance, maybe your friend doesn't reach out to you because they simply don't desire to speak to you as often as you do to them. That's a tough pill to swallow, especially if you're sensitive to rejection (which, honestly, who among us isn't?). But it won't do you any good to go in guns blazing, demanding they call you more. You can't bully or cajole people into wanting to interact with you. I think that's a rule in relationships. So in this case, the best approach would probably be to tend your feelings first. To allow what's there to be there. To be willing. If you do ultimately determine that you want to address an issue with someone, it will be helpful to know what you're feeling, where it comes from, and what you need. Even if it's just to be seen and heard by someone you care about.

The ground that you stand on when you decide to cross the aisle from "this is my stuff" to "this is our stuff" really matters here. When you're coming from a willful place—"I need you to do *this*," "you need to stop doing *that*"—you're kind of inviting suffering, because in most cases you simply don't have that kind of control over what other people do. You can exert your will on other people until the cows come home, but if you haven't tended to your own stuff first you'll wind up lobbing fireballs. And the fact is, people tend to be a lot less receptive with flaming wands flying at them.

Finding the balance between willpower and allowing is much like the image on this card. There is no ground here, not much to hook into that you can take as an absolute reality or guideline. It will require a dogged presence. Just as this image shows eight wands in motion, a photographic capture of a moment that will never look exactly the same again, no two situations will be the same either. But I think that if we make it a guideline to work on our allowing first—what's inside of us and what's inside the world around us—when we do exert will, we can do it with a stance of being grounded in what is. And that's a solid start.

Nine of Wands

ealthy boundaries are like energetic demarcations that separate our thoughts, feelings, and behaviors from the thoughts, feelings, and behaviors of others. This can be hard to grasp if you grew up in an enmeshed system without any such delineations. You may not know what belongs to you and what doesn't, and this murkiness has likely caused you a good deal of confusion and pain.

A thing to know about personal limits is that they can be wildly inconvenient. The situations we like to think of ourselves as equipped for and our actual limitations don't always line up, so at the end of the day, having boundaries is a reality practice. It's an acceptance practice. Bad boundaries often emerge from a wish that we had fewer limits, were more flexible, durable, unfazed. But when a line's been crossed, when you can't bend anymore, when it just doesn't work for you, when it disturbs your work in this world, none of that matters.

Self-help books often define three types of boundaries: porous, rigid, and healthy. In the Nine of Wands, you can see a wall of wands that looks a bit flimsy, if we're honest. The wands are arranged to create a partition, but it's full of gaps. The person who presumably built the wall is ill at ease. While a proper boundary should give us a break from the need to always stand guard, a porous one keeps us incessantly scanning the horizon for incoming threats. With a porous boundary, you don't have a clear sense of where you end and others begin. And I probably don't need to tell you what a toll that can take on one's life force, making little else possible. A strong boundary, on the other hand, frees up energy so that you can focus on restoration and growth.

It's also possible for a boundary to be too strong. A rigid boundary is one where nothing gets in and nothing goes out. It does mitigate the need to constantly scan for threats but makes intimacy and connection impossible in the process. I think it's common to erect rigid boundaries when you've recently realized how long your walls have been porous, and how much that's cost you. The Hermetic principle of rhythm says that it compensates: "The pendulum swing manifests in everything," and that includes boundaries. So if you were too exposed for too long and built an iron fortress around yourself to make up for it, consider the possibility that this might actually mean you're en route to being a person with excellent, healthy boundaries.

Ideally what we want is a boundary that's firm, visible from a mile away but not unwelcoming. There's a doorway through the wall, but the gatekeeper is discerning and has a zero-tolerance policy for nonsense. Maybe it helps to assign a particularly no-nonsense part of yourself to do that job, a part of you that has no qualms about protecting what is precious and that doesn't beat around the bush or mince words when doing so. And then makes a commitment to yield to their counsel.

Though it may feel like just the opposite at first, the best thing you can do to help yourself and others feel safe is to have solid boundaries and uphold them. I often think of communicating a boundary as a bit like getting informed consent from someone. It's right to let others know the terms of engagement before they get involved. This keeps you safe, and it also keeps the other person safe from the possibility of your exploding in a fit of rage because you said yes too many times when you should've said no. It's scary to be close with people who give indiscriminately without a sense of their own limits.

And while coming up against a boundary might be distressing at first for someone who isn't used to boundaries—though they may, and likely will, push back, threaten, stamp their feet, and even punish—I promise you that on some level, even if not immediately apparent, it will make them feel safe. Because they will know exactly what to expect from you.

Ten of Wands

very observable thing on earth has limits around what it requires to sustain itself, even if that limit is as simple as needing water or oxygen to survive. A houseplant needs a certain amount of light and water and will die without them. A skyscraper requires structural components to stay standing when winds are high. Existence is dependent on particular conditions and destruction is promised under others. None of us, try as we may to defy this law of nature, are exempt from it.

I like to think about boundaries as limits, since a limit is something every person has while a boundary can feel like something reserved for only *whole* people, *healthy* people, *people who really have their lives together.* Whether you choose to enforce them or not, you absolutely have limits, lines that should not be crossed. Conditions that are too much or not enough, those that will support your growth or betray it.

A lot of us have grown up in environments where limits are not well understood, acknowledged, or respected. It's not necessarily that the adults in our lives didn't care about our limits; they likely just had trouble recognizing their own and therefore weren't the best teachers of when to say when or of identifying where they ended and another began. Furthermore, if your feelings were routinely dismissed or denied when you were young, or if you were consistently punished for expressing less pleasant emotions like anxiety, fear, anger, or sadness, you might have developed a shell that makes you somewhat numb to your limits. Which you had to be, and that wasn't your fault.

Over years of working with people, I've come to see that difficulty setting boundaries is sometimes a symptom of a sense of oneself that is insubstantial, or that needs fortifying. Not knowing personal limits can stem from a lack of genuine curiosity about one's personal wants, needs, likes, dislikes, values, and morals. In other words, what makes you, you. A boundary is fundamentally about preservation, and setting limits often feels scary. But if our sense of self feels vague or nebulous and it's not clear what we're even trying to protect, we're less likely to be motivated to do the hard work of setting and upholding limits around it in the first place.

A murky self is the kind of self that can be difficult to look out for, but if our parents didn't have a strong sense of who *they* were, we probably didn't come into adulthood with a strong one either. If we weren't encouraged to tend to our personal wants and needs, we may have learned not to take them seriously. And as a result, we might have a hard time as adults knowing what's ours and what's not, which makes it hard to set limits in relationships. Again, when the self is something without clear coordinates, setting limits around it can feel impossible.

The person in the Ten of Wands pushes a heap of wands forward, with their head down and face buried. The human face symbolizes the part of our being that distinguishes us from others; it is how someone else might tell me apart from another tall person with dark hair and olive skin. A burrowed, hidden face implies a person who has not yet completed the psychological task of distinguishing themselves from others. Unable to separate their own wants and needs from the wants and needs of others, they can't tell what is their work and what's not. They take on too much and disregard their limits.

It's tough to say which comes first, the boundaries or the self, but it's safe to say that without a solid sense of self, we will find setting boundaries difficult. So what can be done? I think we can choose to practice behaviors that are boundary clarifying whether we *feel* like it or not, and that will definitely support a budding sense of self. But we'll have to accept that for a while we may not know what it is exactly we're protecting, what makes feeling the guilt, fear, or grief that tends to accompany saying no worthwhile. We can do it anyway.

What else can be done? An investigation of personal limits is probably called for. This is where you shift some of your attention inward rather than always only ever outward, toward the thoughts, feelings, and sensations that arise when you interact with others. This way, you can start to notice what feels good and what doesn't and what it feels like when a limit's been crossed. Ask questions like "How do I know when I've had too much?" and "How do I know when I've not had enough?"

I once overheard my friend Charlie, whom I've mentioned a number of times now, say to a therapy group he was running that people who consistently overextend themselves tend to oscillate between feeling resentful for saying yes and feeling guilty for saying no. As you keep saying yes, he said, resentment keeps building. The more you say no, on the other hand, the more comfortable you get with it, and the guilt that once drove all your yeses starts to gradually subside. This is partly because of how misguided guilt so often is in the first place; it tends to be rooted in conditioning that you're responsible for other people's feelings, which you aren't. This is a charm for anyone on the path toward self-discovery. So if you find yourself standing at the crossroads of guilt and resentment, remember this and see if it aids you.

Page of Wands

The late psychologist James Hillman believed that every person has a purpose that reveals itself in childhood. Due to environmental pressures and family conditioning on the child, this purpose often goes underground, resurfacing later as clusters of mental health symptoms meant to alert the person that they've strayed from the path they were meant for. I haven't thought hard enough about this idea to know whether I agree with it, but I definitely find it to be good food for thought.

Hillman often spoke of the mythic "acorn theory," an idea that suggests we each come into the world with a calling. Rather than being solely under the influence of nature and nurture, the acorn theory teaches that there is in fact something else, something unique about each of us, a part of our being that is connected to our "daemon," which was similar to the Roman concept of genius and the Christian concept of a guardian angel: "Something that you are, that you have, that is not the same as the personality you think you are." According to Hillman, rather than the idea of growing up, the acorn theory spurs us to "grow down," back into alignment with some original, mysterious energy that reminds us who we are.

The Page of Wands represents the energy of youth and the spark of life before it is obscured; when someone says *childlike enthusiasm*, I think this is the energy they're talking about. Children have an innate ability to discern exactly what they like and don't like. If a food tastes, looks, or smells weird, they refuse it. If a piece of clothing is uncomfortable, they reject it, wholeheartedly. Nothing is more ludicrous to a child than wearing something scratchy or stiff. For what? To look like some sort of cherub for the neighbors? Please.

A kid wants to do whatever job sounds the coolest and most interesting: astronaut, paleontologist, teacher. They're not concerning themselves with salary, benefits, or PTO. When asked what they want to eat for dinner, they're not thinking about sodium levels or calories. They're thinking about what's going to feel good and taste good. What's going to fulfill a desire in that moment. I can't tell you how many adults I've worked with who couldn't identify a true desire if they tried. To be tapped into this energy is to be available for what truly excites, vivifies, and moves us, and I think this is what Hillman was driving at when he spoke of growing down. In the words of mythologist Martin Shaw, as adults, too many of us have become "heavily defended against experiences of our own beauty."

All of the pages in tarot—the Page of Wands, the Page of Cups, the Page of Pentacles, the Page of Swords—symbolize youth, innocence, and wonder. Just as a child has endless questions about the world, the Page of Wands wants us to ask ourselves, What do I love? What captivates my attention? What grips me, lights me up, claims me? The Page of Wands is an invitation to reconnect with something raw and original within us, something many of us relinquish as we cross the threshold into adulthood.

I like to think about the Page of Wands as the keeper of a little spark that lives inside each of us. And though that spark sometimes gets obscured or covered over by judgments, core beliefs, and social pressures, the Page of Wands bears that spark as long as we are alive. Conceptually similar to Hillman's idea of the daemon, this page could be seen as a sort of guide, one assigned to us at birth and who might act up when we stray too far from the thing we're meant to do in the world.

Perhaps, tucked inside the things we are brave enough to love with reckless abandon, there is a specific calling and purpose that, even as we can (and very often do) veer woefully out of alignment with, is never far from reach. And even if our judgments, core beliefs, social pressures, and demands of life under capitalism grow big and run rampant in the hallways of our conscious awareness, covering the trailhead of the path toward what we came to do, the path is still there. However hidden.

Rudimentary as it may sound, finding our way back to that spark of the things we truly love can be deceptively challenging in a world that banks on our forgetting. But when you've made contact with that spark even once, you will know. And if you listen closely, the wands suit will show you how to cup your hand around that spark and keep it safe so that with it you can warm not only yourself but whole villages.

Knight of Wands

lchemists often used the triangle to symbolize fire. This was, according to historian of art and the occult Fred Gettings, to represent that "the fire principle strives upwards, as though to the spiritual realm. The broad base of the triangle also indicates that the creative force of fire is well founded or stable, resting firmly and securely on the earth." I see this concept of upward motion depicted in the image of the Knight of Wands, whose horse is bucking, back on two legs. There's no shortage of fire, but a stable base is what the Knight of Wands appears to be missing.

There are two folk interpretations that stand out in my mind about the Knight of Wands, and they are either that something's about to get upended or that someone's afraid of commitment. I don't like hard-and-fast rules for interpretation, but I often use the stages of change model to work with the court cards (the page, the knight, the queen, and the king); while the page is in a contemplation phase, thinking about making a change and feeling inspired to do so, the knight is pulling together resources and taking action, as symbolized by the fact that all the knights in tarot are on horseback. Movement is happening.

The Knight of Wands' wild and unbridled appearance here might not sync up with our mental image of "preparing and taking appropriate action." But in truth, this is what making change often looks and feels like. If the wands suit relates to a spark of vitality in each of us, and the change we're making is about reestablishing our connection to that often elusive but transformative flame—the one that drives creativity, fuels passion, and gives meaning to our lives—the Knight of Wands tells us, first off, this might need to get a bit messy.

An understanding of the Knight of Wands as having to do with breaking up stagnation is also relevant here. When it feels like you're locked inside an ice house, the emphasis should be less on the specific dance steps you're doing to stay alive and more on the fact that you're dancing at all because movement is what's going to generate heat, heat is what's going to get the ice house walls melting, and melting is what's going to keep you alive. It might be a while of just doing weird random dances, watching diligently for the walls to start sweating, and relentlessly praying that a patch of sky will poke through. A degree of faith in the unseen is needed; that's a big message in the wands suit.

And this is also where the idea of the Knight of Wands as relating to commitment comes into play: When people who've felt stuck a long time finally do take action to get unstuck, they sometimes get so comfortable busting up routines that it creates a new kind of stuckness in reaction to the terror of getting stuck ever again. They start to see everything stable as an ice house and conflate security with being confined, so they dance endlessly. But without any grounding, like a triangle without a base, they float up and away, become lost.

Understanding the stages of change can help to normalize what you might be experiencing at a given point in your process. Often when you're trying to get to a more masterful place with something, you have to bear looking foolish and out of control for a while. No one else needs to understand it. You yourself probably don't even need to understand it. In that early process of reconnecting with our spark, whatever it is that will thaw the frozen parts of our lives and give our days warmth again, we could get carried away, go overboard. We might fan the flames too much and torch the nourishment. That's how we learn, with time, to harness fire in order to feed ourselves for the long haul. To recognize the difference between a flame that is nourishing and one that is destructive. To tell when we're running toward something specific from when we're simply on the run.

Queen of Wands

hat words are right to describe the Queen of Wands, queen of fire, the element described by Aleister Crowley as "so kin to Spirit that it is not a substance at all, but a phenomenon, yet so integral to Matter that it is the very heart and essence of all things soever." This is the queen of spirit and of the energy that animates. A true guardian of flame.

For those characters in the tarot who are especially resistant to being placed in boxes, I've found it helpful to ground them in some sort of context, tracking them back to where they've shown up in stories. In Greek mythology, Hestia is known as the goddess of the hearth—symbol of both home and nourishment, the stuff that forms the base of the triangle that the Knight of Wands was missing. The hearth is, of course, the space where fire, the alchemical symbol of spirit, resides, and it is also the place where, in ancient Greece, all offerings to the gods were made. Though Hestia was a bit of an unsung hero in Greek mythology, by some accounts she held a seat among the twelve ruling Olympians, alongside the likes of Zeus, Poseidon, Apollo, and Aphrodite.

In ancient Greece, many offerings to gods involved fire, and so Hestia, while understated, was so revered that she was said to have received the first and last offerings at any meal. Hearth spaces, whether private or public, were something to be protected. The fires in them were required to be maintained at all times, and failure to do so was considered immoral. And so Hestia, as guardian of this flame, was the Greeks' connection to nourishment—since fire is how people cooked

meals—warmth, and light, but also to the other gods, since every offering made went through her. Without the hearth, there was no food,
no warmth, no light, and no way of communicating with the Divine.

Some say smoke carries prayers to the heavens, which makes it
easy to see how the wand, symbol of fire, is also a symbol of that which
unites above and below. And so the Queen of Wands asks questions
about how we nourish ourselves and others, how we generate warmth
and light, and how ultimately these practices keep us linked with something greater.

Joseph Campbell famously talked about the importance of having
a sacred space and time where you don't know what's on the news,
what your friends are doing, or what's on your to-do list that day, but
rather you simply find a way to ground and make an opening for creativity. A lot of us don't have fireplaces in our homes, or proper hearths,
but it feels as though Campbell was suggesting we create something to
serve that same function, a place where we protect and guard the flame
of our creative spirit and come into conversation with the symbolic
gods, whether our gods be things like personal values, moral or spiritual codes, or deities with the ability to influence our lives on earth.

If you've ever been tasked with building or keeping a fire going
without kerosene or lighter fluid, you probably already carry some of
the fire queen's secrets. To build and maintain a slow and steady burn,
a proper burn, requires knowledge, dedication, and the right materials.
If you can get a little fire going using some tiny bits of wood and paper—
I'm talking shreds here—you're laying a foundation for a bigger fire.
Our creative lives are often what nourish and illuminate our lives
through the nights and winters. So if you journal every day for ten
years, you may be lighting the coals for the memoir you'll write later,
or for whatever it is that you think of as your "real" work.

As with most things, there are shortcuts to getting a big fire going—
lighter fluid, for example—but relying on these circumvents a crucial
part of the process, which is the part where you either dig for hot coals
under the ash to get something going, or have to start from what feels
like scratch, putting a spark to cold ground and building slowly from
there. Even though the old stories are full of cases where a charm is

given that offers a magical shortcut or a throughway from nowhere to somewhere, it still seems to me that there is inherent value in taking the slow way. Putting the time in to learn something without some supernatural aid.

I can't explain why but it just *feels* like there's meaning in learning to make something from nothing, in walking that path from the Page of Wands to the Queen of Wands, where you start with a spark that you have to cup your hand around to keep lit and arrive eventually to a place where the fire in your life—the stuff that inspires, tells you that you're alive, even reminds you what you're uniquely here to do—burns steady. If for no other reason than because then, when it goes out, you'll know how to bring it back again.

King of Wands

aron Beck, the founder of cognitive behavioral therapy (CBT), used the term *hot cognitions* to refer to the emotion-laden psychological experiences that often bring people to therapy in the first place. In sessions, cognitive behavioral therapists will sometimes actively elicit hot cognitions as a way to call up the material that activates people most, in order to see what's there and find new ways of working with it. They do this not to be cruel, but because just like the alchemical fire, hot cognitions contain within them some of the most potent material for transformation.

As an alchemist might burn a substance first in order to clear off what was not "real," psychological heat does something similar to the human experience. Anger, passion, despair, and intense conflict are all experiences that burn away our defenses and melt the veneer of our "civilized" selves. Fire has been called a judge, in that it determines what stays and what goes, what is worthy of survival and what should or must be destroyed.

Jungian analyst Marie-Louise von Franz has gone so far as to say that if an analysand "does not suffer—if there is neither the fire of despair nor hatred nor conflict nor fury nor annoyance nor anything of that kind—one can be pretty sure that not much will be constellated and it will be a blah-blah analysis forever." And so even if the fire is a destructive force in a person's life, it has the potential within it to be a catalyst for maturing. One of the most often noted features of the King of Wands is his restless energy. As a king is a symbol of something exalted, fire in its highest function always has a job to do. To keep burning away and burning away to vapor what is not true. A lifetime of work, for sure.

Having identified the value in hot cognitions, what does one do with such material exactly, in order to *use* that fire rather than allow it to rage wild or uncontained? First of all, pay attention to the moments when you've behaved in a way that you wished you hadn't. You canceled plans to go to a party because you were too anxious about socializing. You picked a fight with your partner because they said something earlier that stimulated a fear of abandonment. You wrote an angry email to someone that you wish you'd sat with awhile longer.

What was passing through your heart, mind, and body in those moments? If, when you go to recall what you did, you feel detached, there's nothing hot there; you're working with an energy that's not going to be of much use to this process. But if you can find some orange coal that really singes, something that makes you want to hide your face in shame, or rage like a wildfire at 0 percent containment, well, now you're cooking. Now you're in alchemist territory. And if you're brave enough to go into these spaces, you're activating the part of you that lives to transmute, that's big King of Wands energy.

You may be wondering why we're talking about cognition in the wands suit, when wands relate to energy. I actually think that the term *hot cognition* is much more a way of talking about something energetic than intellectual, it's a response to what might be called our "intuitive appraisal" of something, that is, our raw experience before our thoughts and defenses kick in. To connect with this molten stuff, we usually have to circumvent the swords of the intellect and the stories we tell that keep us from connecting with what needs our attention.

Don't be surprised if you have a hard time accessing hot material. A lot of us learned that it was wrong to feel the things we did, so when we go to recall something like intense anger or despair, we often encounter a psychological defense—"I had no business feeling that way"—that blocks us from feeling it. In this case, the cause is not lost but rather redirected; your work can be to poke around and uncover where it was that you learned it was not okay to feel certain things. And try not to be shocked if, in doing so, you touch something hot.

Therapists use questions to dig for coals under the ashes of time and conditioning, and when they do, they'll sometimes ask clients to play the role of the irrational part of themselves. The part that doesn't say, "I know it's childish," "I know this sounds juvenile," and "I know it's ridiculous, but..." This is one instance where that noble, neutral, nonjudgmental feeling is actually *not* what you're going for. The more fiery, the more irrational, the more unreasonable, the better. You want to get underneath the part of you that knows not to feel something, past the scope of logic, down to the burning ember in your heart and mind. That's King of Wands territory and it is, in the words of ethnobotanist Terence McKenna, "where the alchemist loves to begin."

Ace of Cups

In the West we tend to see emotions as insular experiences that exist within individuals, an isolated phenomenon that is mine, yours, or someone else's. But I often wonder, especially when working with the cups suit—the suit of water—whether we've fundamentally misunderstood this domain of our experience.

Once, humans understood psyche or the soul not as something that existed within the individual but rather as something the individual existed inside. Old ways took for granted that internal life and external life were linked, but today we seem to have forgotten about that. Our narratives usually sound like this. *What have I done, what can I do, what should I do to influence the world around me.* We rarely ask and get quiet enough to hear what our environments might be expressing through us.

The cups suit is linked with the High Priestess, who is sometimes read as having to do with the practice of contemplation. We tend to think of contemplation as having to do with thinking, but it is really more a creative process of coming into dialogue with other forces, such as emotions. The prefix con-, meaning "with," tells us that it's a collaborative process, and *templum*, the Latin word for temple, connotes a sacred space where a deity was believed to reside. And so to contemplate is to engage in spiritual dialogue, which, like all dialogues, is going to involve both speaking and listening. What you're listening for might be an invisible force, like that of helping spirits, energetic currents, or a Higher Power. Or you could be listening for something concrete, like a river over rocks, birdsong, or a groundhog's rustle through high grass. This way of being in a receptive relationship with what surrounds us seems difficult for modern people of the West to understand. We think in terms of the individual, the hero, the character who performs tasks and overcomes obstacles.

But the cups, in addition to being emotional, are also symbolic of a certain receptivity, as a cup receives water. Receptivity implies relationship and asks us: What would a more relational way of engaging with our surroundings look like? What would happen if we reoriented the imagination toward a way that sees the self both as dreamer and that which is dreamt? Could we make room for the possibility that what we feel and experience in the flesh house of the body is not always rooted in a private individual experience, but comes from an ecosystem to which we belong? What if, for example, rather than seeing ourselves as taking a walk through the woods, we see ourselves as being a wave of energy rippling through the consciousness of a family of redwoods? How would this change the way we move through the environments we dwell in? How would it change the way we relate to our experiences?

Emotions are how we understand our raw experiences, not in an evaluative or judgmental way as with intellectual understanding but rather as an intuitive, felt, cellular-type knowing. The trick—and what's taught in many behavioral therapies—is learning to suspend action for long enough that this kind of knowing can move through us.

In her Dear Sugar column, Cheryl Strayed once advised a reader, "Don't own other people's crap." And I've thought about that a lot over the years. To understand the cups suit, we have to get clear on what aspects of our experience even fall into the realm of ownership. For example, my behavior is something I can "own" or be accountable for, while other people's behavior is not something that I can or should. But with emotions, it's not always clear who "owns" them. I've woken up heavy with the boulder of my grandmother's grief on my chest, breathed deeply while sweating from the fire of my mother's rage, and I could say, "That's theirs, not mine," if I wanted to, but what good would that do? Emotions are living energetic currents with life cycles of their own. They tend to survive down the vertical and horizontal lines of human relationships—through generations, through communities—until they arrive to the place where they can be fully experienced and expressed. That can take a while.

It seems to me that when an emotion arrives, it's yours to deal with, regardless of where it came from. If a storm comes and floods your house, would you search for whom the water belonged to and then send the nearest large body of water a bill for the damage? When the house floods, it is inconsequential which body of water or whose territory it was where the rain clouds formed. No one asks, no one cares. If you're in it, it's yours to deal with.

If we understand magic as using the subtle to influence the dense, we can listen to the way that the subtle, invisible energy of emotions moves through us and others, often intermingling in the intrapsychic space. We can open ourselves up to the forces that are trying to be expressed through us and maybe learn to take it a bit less personally. So often our problems in the emotional space stem from beliefs that grief means we did something wrong or that if we're angry, we ought to be ashamed. We don't have to look at it this way. Emotions come from all kinds of places; we can be like the cup and make a space to receive them.

The Ace of Cups is often depicted as the Holy Grail, the cup sought after by knights in the legends of western Europe. The Holy Grail was alleged to have magical healing powers and was believed by some to be the cup that Jesus drank from at the Last Supper. In the story of the Holy Grail, the protagonist Percival attains it when—and only when—he arrives at the Grail castle and asks the wounded king guarding the Grail: "What ails you?" Neither chivalry nor courage nor cunning were required—it is this simple asking, this *receptivity*, that ultimately earns Percival the prize. The lesson here, I think, is that taking the time to be curious about emotions—to ask questions, to listen, to be receptive—is the key to attaining something holy and treasured.

Two of Cups

Projection is the unconscious transfer of one's own thoughts, motivations, desires, or feelings to another person. It can be both beneficial and problematic. For instance, it's a lot more common to go into a relationship projecting a fantasy of what we hope to see onto the other person than it is to go in actively looking at who that person truly is and then determining the viability of a match from there.

The Two of Cups holds an image of two people staring at each other, as if looking into a mirror. The mirror metaphor speaks to the ways that what we see when we look at another person is so often generated by our core beliefs about relationships: our minds are always pattern matching, seeking evidence that the dynamics we learned in childhood are how it is in all relationships thereafter. Think about how often, when it comes to gripes you've had with partners, the same could be said verbatim about issues you've had with a parent or caregiver. "You always make it about you," "you never listen to me," "stop trying to control me." Think about how often it is that the "you" you're referring to is actually the person whose job it was to take care of you growing up.

Projection doesn't only happen in arguments and moments of discord. When a relationship feels harmonious or blissful (I sometimes think bliss—especially early on in relationships—might be a dead giveaway that projection is happening) it's not that we're not projecting, it's just that our fantasies happen to be compatible and exquisitely well-timed. It's when we break from others' projections of us, or they break from ours, that things get hairy and often ugly; feelings of betrayal, abandonment, and disappointment emerge. We've projected our earliest unmet needs onto a partner, and for a while they appear to be able to meet them. But then they break from that script, diverge from the psychic blueprint we'd laid over them, and now the honeymoon's over. Hearts grow frightened and contract, relationships dissolve, people part ways.

Psychologist Edward Teyber wrote that one of the primary psychological tasks in early marriage counseling is to help couples relinquish their projections and distortions about each other. To get to know who each other really is, to behold what is there and not hover merely inches apart from each other, reaching out our hands but never really touching. I don't have any marriage counseling experience, but here's the wisdom I gathered from Teyber's comments: Be curious. Ask questions. Watch your assumptions. Take the time to explore what you're hoping for based on your deepest yearnings from childhood until today, and then seek reality in what's being offered as much as possible.

Another way that projection happens is when feelings basically move invisibly from one person to another. Person A "projects" a feeling—like rage or shame that they're not able or willing to claim—onto Person B by behaving, usually unconsciously, in a way that will stimulate those same feelings in the other person. Person B suddenly feels inexplicably angry or ashamed. One reason we might do this—it's called projective identification—is that it allows us to engage with strong feelings that we're unequipped to claim or own by giving them to and then experiencing them through the people around us. This way, we can still make contact with them from a manageable distance without having to claim or work through them ourselves. These invisible trades we do with people we're close to are sometimes copacetic, and sometimes deeply problematic. In the latter case, it's helpful to do a bit of exploration. What are *they* always doing, feeling, or expressing, according to you? And is it possible that any of that stuff is actually yours?

I think it's worth noting that emotions aren't like possessions in the material world in that they may not "belong" to one person or another. We can and do give our emotions to others all the time, through unconscious behaviors that trigger the feelings in other people that we're not able to tolerate (think about the insecure person in relationships who deliberately tries to make their partner jealous) and generationally, as we unwittingly pass down to our kids and grandkids what we didn't have the resources to process.

So projection is two things. It's laying a fantasy over someone and expecting them to live up to that fantasy, and it's "giving" emotional experiences to others that we need, for whatever reason, to disassociate ourselves from. Water is an apt symbol for emotion in part because, like the archetypal trickster, it is slippery in the way that it can penetrate walls and boundaries invisibly, going from over here to over there without ever being seen. So here are some clues that projection is happening: the intensity level of the emotions evoked seems disproportionate to the perceived offense; you feel hopelessly hooked into an intimate relationship with someone and seem unable to free yourself; you are inexplicably drawn to someone who is completely incompatible with your life goals; you are (seemingly) irrationally irked or disgusted by someone; you have a "type," such as the emotionally or physically unavailable, depressed, or rageful.

And though projection gets a bad rap, psychotherapist David Richo writes that these products of the relational imagination "show us that other people are not out there as totally other. They are reflections/projections of our own story. They are part of us. They are not only 'they'... but also 'I.'" And perhaps that's why the intensity we feel for and toward people seems to magically shift and fade as we ask about and attend to our own wounds.

Three of Cups

During my second year of graduate school, I worked as an intern therapist for the outpatient mental health department at a community hospital outside of Philadelphia. The dialectical behavioral therapy (DBT) team would gather once a week to review DBT concepts and provide consultation for one another on some of their more challenging cases.

DBT was developed in the 1970s by a suicide researcher, and its focus on mindfulness, interpersonal effectiveness, emotion regulation, and distress tolerance has been shown to be particularly helpful for people struggling with self-harming and suicidal behaviors and those who often experience psychological crises. I learned a lot about how to support people in crisis as an intern in that DBT group. One week, as I listened to the therapists talk about the nuances of responding to crisis, I learned something that took me a bit by surprise: sometimes, the way we respond to those who are suffering can actually reinforce the very thing we're hoping to prevent.

For instance, when people receive attention and care during times of suffering but are ignored or disregarded all the rest of the time, they are receiving a powerful message that being in pain is the best way to get their needs met. In those cases, it really should come as no surprise when someone stays suffering. Unconscious "resistance" to getting better and being well—because of a fear that the care one has come to rely on will be withdrawn if they do—is a very real thing. Not just in clinical settings, but also in families, friend groups, romantic relationships, and communities.

Of course, when people we care about are suffering, our withholding care in fear of sending the message that suffering and the provision of care go hand in hand would be inappropriate. So what should we do? A DBT therapist might say that we should practice reinforcing experiences of wellness by offering attention and care in those times, too, thus communicating that care is available in both the depths and the heights. The Three of Cups depicts three people dancing, holding one another up in their joy, reinforcing it. How do we do that? How do we ensure that we're there for loved ones in their suffering, but also that we reinforce their well-being?

Life is busy, and it's easy to stay in reactivity. Putting out fires. Attending only to what needs immediate relief and nothing more. That doesn't seem good or sustainable if we're hoping to build futures that are healthy and happy and certainly not without suffering, but not built around it either. Maybe we can try to keep in mind that, as social beings, attention from our fellow humans is a powerful motivator. And that whether we receive that attention because we are in pain or in need, or because we are thriving and joyous, being tended to by others communicates something deep in the fibers of our being. It's common to have relationships that are rooted in the mutual reinforcement of pain and suffering, and I believe that it's also possible to have the same with joy and ease.

It's considered best practice in friendship to call a friend after they've experienced a painful loss, but how often are we calling our friends just to hear the ins and outs of a recent promotion or a new art project they're working on that they're clearly excited about? Maybe this is the essence of what's behind a congratulatory Hallmark card or a high school graduation party: the reinforcement of thriving. But I think we could get a lot more creative in coming up with new, better, and more potent ways to encourage and hold each other up in our joy.

Four of Cups

The Four of Cups is one of those strange cards that seems to tell me a different secret every time we meet. Given that the number four often connotes stability and the cups relate to water, the fact that the basis of this card would be prone to shape-shifting, as water does depending on the vessel it's poured into, makes sense. All of the cards are like this to an extent, but this one especially.

The person seated at the base of this tree could be resting, meditating, processing, or procrastinating, or they might just be plain bored. I've read interpretations that say this card is about self-absorption and stubbornness. I've seen it have to do with a lack of receptivity. To discern meaning in any situation demands that we tune our ears to hear the truth of what's being expressed. The cards give us a microcosm within which to practice the ideal that when listening, we should take nothing for granted. Every detail matters and provides a line into something potentially significant. Here, we see three cups on the ground. A person is staring at them, with their arms folded across their chest. A fourth cup is being handed to this person out of the sky, but it appears they're not really open to receiving it. What's this about?

I think about this card as having to do with the human problem that we've forgotten how to listen. The comforts of domesticated life require less attunement than ever before, and the more comforts we have, the less we need to rely on cues from the world around us. Our rusty listening skills are sometimes evident in the experience of working with the raw imagery of a card itself and not knowing how to understand its language. We engage with tarot cards the way we engage with a lot of other things in this world—as objects to support our agendas and bolster our polemics. Not as entities unto themselves that would offer something if we only knew how to listen. I think that, among other things, this is a card about not listening.

We're constantly projecting our inner worlds—beliefs, desires, fantasies—onto the world around us. We decide what we want to eat for dinner without considering what's in season. We build homes in areas that are not meant for human habitation. We extract natural resources without ever stopping to ask what we can give back unless giving back means we'll ultimately get more. Sometimes not even then.

Often even when we think we're giving, we're taking. We give to make ourselves feel good, to feel aligned with the belief that we are righteous, and to be perceived by others as virtuous. When we give, how often are we doing so based on a real assessment of what's needed or actually being asked for? Maybe we clip a sprig of rosemary from a bush and offer a quick prayer or blessing to show our gratitude to the plant. Did the bush ask for that? If it had asked for something, would you have heard it? Did it even occur to you to listen? Or do you move through life taking, with your arms across your chest?

Maybe it's less that we don't want or know how to be receptive, and more that we're just scared to be. We're scared to let go of our agenda and listen for what wants to happen. We don't know how to tolerate the emotional reality of things not going our way. Sometimes we feel safer projecting our imaginings of how things ought to be, crossing our fingers and praying for the best. Even though so very often that way creates suffering. But what if there were another way? A way where we could listen for what's being offered, uncross our arms, hold out our hands, and accept it?

Five of Cups

olk interpretations of the Five of Cups point out that the person depicted in the card is so concerned with the three spilled cups that they've neglected the two still standing. This can certainly be read as a metaphor for the power of perspective and the difference it can have on how we experience and move forward from a situation. The point is often made that if they could just turn around, the person in this card would see opportunity rather than loss.

But I think we miss out on something crucial if we don't first learn to look squarely at the cups that have spilled. Sure, if we look too long, we might turn to stone, or get stuck in self-pity, self-criticism, or despair. But maybe the trick is to recognize that we actually have the capacity to both look at and learn from. We can feel the full impacts of a situation—a misstep or backslide that led to a deeply painful experience or tragic loss, perhaps—and then we can let the material and emotional consequences teach us. Having felt the full weight of a painful thing, we can turn on our heel and move forward with an equal level of fullness, maybe even toward a gift. Feeling the repercussions of our behaviors initiates us into the space where we can learn to do better.

Shame makes it difficult to do this. People who struggle with compulsive behavior often experience intense shame after doing a habitual thing that they swore they'd stop doing. The intensity of the shame around the "forbidden" behavior stimulates an avoidance response that makes the person unable to look directly at or feel into a misstep and its aftermath. Shame is an experience of not only having *done something* bad but actually *being* bad, and it's often rooted in old, early learning. But shame restricts our ability to turn around and look at what's happened from the perspective that every "mistake" is an opportunity to learn. Research has shown that compassion is a good medicine for shame because it doesn't require that we like or love ourselves to extend kindness, only that we notice our suffering and feel motivated to alleviate it. Taking a hard look at our mistakes so that we can see the ways we might be able to suffer less next time is a good first step to reducing unnecessary pain in the long term.

But if we can't look straight down the barrel of our mistakes—at the feelings, bodily sensations, and thoughts that have come up in their wake—we rob ourselves of a precious opportunity to gain a depth of understanding around why, on a felt level, the behavior is no good for us. In Jamaica there is a saying: "Who feels it, knows it." That wisdom is perfect here.

Looking at a behavior that we feel ashamed about gives us room to explore what led to the behavior, what might have triggered it, and what was happening internally or externally at the time. If the behavior was in response to a difficult emotion, this will also give us the option to identify some other coping skills to use instead next time, rather than continue to do that same old thing we hate doing, and start to build new skills for managing our emotions and tolerating distress. If we can't look because we're caught in shame-driven avoidance, we can't learn.

Six of Cups

rthur Waite wrote that the Six of Cups is "a card of the past and of memories, looking back, as—for example—on childhood." It is often interpreted as a card about nostalgia and sweetness.

It makes sense that nostalgia belongs in the cups suit. The cups are linked with water, water linked with life, life linked with creation. Creativity is a process of life giving; it's how we carve out space to give life to something, or to preserve life lost. Mythologist Martin Shaw has described art as "a dignified display of the heartbreak which is the debt of living." And this is where the nostalgia comes in. Creative work is a ritual effort to experience something as enduring through the harsh and unforgiving dimensions of passing time. I don't use the word *ritual* loosely here, but to describe the summoning and recalling of very particular emotional states and of marking those states in time and space, to remember.

Benedictine monk David Steindl-Rast has written that "the intellect sifts out what is true; the will reaches out for what is good. But there is a third dimension to reality: beauty. Our whole being resonates with what is beautiful." When we experience beauty, he wrote, we start to speak about emotions, and the more we are touched on an emotional level, the more we seek to celebrate the experience, and it's there that we begin to create ritual. He wrote that all rituals have to do with, and celebrate, belonging.

In the context of the Six of Cups, we might think of ritual as a thing we do to mark, remember, and reenact experiences of emotional resonance from the past. Maybe it's returning to gaze over the same vistas or reciting the same prayers. Maybe it's a behavior you discovered long ago could soothe or calm you and so it became ritualistic, ceremonial even. The things we do again and again can commemorate or replicate emotional states from the past for better or for worse. If long ago you did something and felt safe or powerful as a result, it would make sense that out of a yearning to return to that feeling, you made a ritual of it. Did it again and again and again and again and again. You made of it what Steindl-Rast calls a "personal holy place."

The reframing of repetitive behaviors as ritual, and of ritual as the behavioral practice of preserving and commemorating experiences of beauty, belonging, or any other desired emotional state, is powerful for many reasons. So many rituals are stigmatized, seen primarily as moral failings, called by words like *dysfunctional, maladaptive, unhealthy, not serving you*, and so on. But as far as I know, the way behavior works is we don't do things that don't serve us in some way.

The tenderness in the image of the Six of Cups tells a secret. What if—instead of beating ourselves up for the things we do over and over again that we wish we didn't—we saw these behaviors as highly intelligent? As the creation of rituals that would mark, preserve, and facilitate a return to emotional experiences that are sacred to us. If we could validate that, in a terrifying world, to feel safe is sacred. To be soothed is sacred. This way, maybe we could understand—like water running beneath earth *stands under* an aboveground layer that is more than what it appears—why we do what we do before we start in with the judgments. Instead of calling ourselves stuck or hopeless or lost, we could call ourselves lovers of beauty and of belonging, lovers of deep emotional resonance just trying to recall some sacred feeling. And then maybe, if necessary, we could begin to explore new ways to recall those same feelings, new rituals for feeling safe and soothed.

Seven of Cups

he imagination is so powerful that it can not only stimulate intense feelings from thin air, if we don't know how to work with those feelings, but also drive behavior, which can change the physical reality of our lives. Let's say someone has done something that I imagine is an intentional attack on me. As a result of this imagined attack, I become furious. I fire off an angry text to this person that I can't unsend. Unbeknownst to me, the person has just lost a loved one suddenly, and they've acted the way they had toward me not out of malice, but because they were in shock.

So a chain reaction has happened: my imagination stimulated feelings that in turn triggered an action. With awareness and practice, we can definitely get less reactive to feelings and better at making space between intense internal events and behavior, but I'd venture to guess that even with dedication, most of us will never be entirely free from doing this. A testament to the power of imagination, for better or worse. And it's such an important thing to recognize because once you are aware of it, you can start learning how to harness it. Instead of imagining a situation in which the worst thing happens, why not imagine scenarios in which you are taking good care of yourself, making space for things to go wrong, and having everything you need to manage.

The Seven of Cups depicts a person standing before seven cups, not one. There is a choice implied here. And while you can't direct your imagination all the time, sometimes you can. If you pull this card, why not take whatever you're consulting the cards about and come up with an alternative ending where the best possible thing happens, instead of the worst. Instead of imagining an outcome you don't like, substitute it for one that involves grace, compassion, and power.

That's one amazing thing about the mind. You have the ability to summon, through your imagination, whatever world you want. And if you're able to direct that capacity with intention, it can radically change your physical reality. Because that same psychological muscle that imagines worst-case scenarios and stimulates a whole heap of feelings about it can imagine best possible outcomes and stimulate sweet feelings, too. Which can in turn stimulate the best and sweetest behaviors.

Eight of Cups

everal years ago I was sitting at a dinner table with a bunch of psychologists during a behavioral science conference that I got to go to because I worked for the press that published their books. Someone at the table whose work focuses on quick interventions to help people change told me that because so many clients never come back to therapy after the first session, you have to go into every meeting with the assumption that it may be your last. Which brought us to an exploration of the question: If you knew you had only one session with a client experiencing stuckness, what would you want them to leave with from that time? If I had to choose one thing, I think I'd focus on coping skills.

I spend a lot of time thinking about how people get stuck in the wrong situations, doing things for too long that aren't working for them and in some cases actually harming themselves and others in the process. I don't believe in catchall approaches to anything really, but for sure one thing that keeps a great deal of people stuck in bad situations is that deep down they don't believe they can cope with the feelings that walking away will require: grief, loneliness, anxiety, fear, stress, rejection, anger, despair, and so on. This means that it's not enough to convince someone that what they're doing isn't working, and it's often not enough to convince ourselves of this, either, if the coping skills aren't there to support the change.

By and large, people who know they will be okay no matter what happens are more willing to walk away when walking away is called for. They know they'll be okay because they have skills for coping, a kind of psychic insurance to cover the incidentals of moving freely through life rather than staying stuck in the driveway when you're supposed to be somewhere.

The Eight of Cups depicts an image of a person walking away from eight shining cups, beautiful and vibrant and valuable in certain ways, but not enough—that not-enough-ness implied by the gap in the stack where a ninth cup would go. This card is often interpreted as a difficult departure, a walking away that requires faith (there is no destination pictured), intuition (there is no path), and also what is not visible—the fact that this person has the ability to cope with whatever it takes to walk while carrying the weight of losing the eight cups they've left behind.

Reading tarot cards, you work with a lot of people asking various forms of the question "Should I stay or should I go?" Through the years I've noticed that there are very few people for whom intellectual awareness that they should leave is enough to convince them to leave. The cups in this card suggest that in order to complete the difficult task of walking away, we need to develop a level of skill in working with our emotions. Healthy coping skills are like a protective talisman or charm that you can draw from your back pocket in the moment when it becomes necessary to break your own heart.

Knowing how to cope well with the requisite pain and grief of letting go is hugely important when making a life. It is foundational to getting unstuck because it diminishes the compulsion to cope in ways that make things worse. It's also often only when people build adequate coping skills that suppressed material is able to emerge to be integrated—all the stuff that refusing change allows us to avoid—and this is also an important part of healing. When we have the coping skills to manage the emotional windfall of tough choices, we can do hard things rather than live our lives avoiding feelings we don't have the tools to manage. Because paradoxically, avoidance makes life exponentially less manageable as time goes on. Coping skills are a basic competency for the tough calls that a good life requires.

Nine of Cups

I do a lot of tarot readings for people who are trying to figure out what they want. In therapy, values clarification is often an early task in the process, the idea being that in order for a person to be motivated to do the hard work of making changes in their life, they'll likely need to have a sense of what will make the hard work worth it. Values are defined in acceptance and commitment therapy (ACT) as having to do with what gives our life meaning and purpose, and are used as a sort of compass that we can always check in with to see whether we're moving toward or away from what's precious.

Knowing what you want is often deceptively challenging. The Nine of Cups, commonly read as being a card about wish fulfillment, invites us to explore what we truly desire. This can be hard for many reasons, one being how often the physical reality of our lives doesn't line up with what we desire, and so to accept what we want requires us also to accept the pain of not having it. And though values clarification is a process that typically happens early in therapy, I've found that identifying what's personally meaningful and articulating desires from that place is often in and of itself a whole healing process.

As we saw with the Chariot and Strength cards, to move through life as though it were an obstacle course, completing tasks assigned to us by others, is one thing. But to turn inward—when turning inward has never been invited let alone encouraged or rewarded—to determine what is of true value requires something else of us entirely. Making a wish sounds like fun until you realize you have no idea what you want. Until you realize you're not even sure what it feels like to truly want something and are not convinced you'd know it if you felt it. This experience of finding a void where a wish ought to be can be profoundly distressing.

I say this to normalize not knowing what you want because I've seen what shame it can bring up. I can't tell you how many times I've heard, through the choking back of tears, something along the lines of "I'm twenty-three years old," "I'm fifty-six years old," "I am one hundred and fifty-seven years old," followed by "I should know who I am by now." The shame isn't going to get you any closer to knowing what to wish for, and luckily there's a good medicine for shame: self-compassion. Not knowing what you want is often rooted in things that weren't your choice and aren't your fault. Here are some reasons why making a wish might be hard:

Your feelings were constantly invalidated in childhood so you don't trust your own sense of what you like and long for.

You've experienced a lot of frustration trying to get your needs met in life, which makes it difficult to want to try. Feeling hopeless about or quickly shutting down anything you have an inkling of really wanting is how you've learned to feel safe.

The people you relied on in childhood were unpredictable or erratic, so you developed the skill of scanning and tending to other people's needs at the expense of your own. This created an experience of your own needs as being necessarily dictated by the needs of others, so it's hard to untangle them.

You developed a protective strategy commonly known as perfectionism, which means you organize your life around avoiding contact with any potential indications of being inadequate, defective, or unlovable. Wishing for or trying new things is a direct threat to that defense.

When you were growing up, no one around you had any coping skills, so you didn't get any, either, and instead carry an intense fear of the feelings that come with wanting something and not getting it. Fused with a belief that those feelings are unmanageable, the stakes of having a true wish are simply too high.

A heart's desire sprouts from a sense of self that's sturdy enough to have preferences independent of external factors. In other words, when we know who we are, we can appropriately weigh our internal wants and needs against the wants and needs of the whole. There are so many factors that go into the maturation of a budding sense of self, and probably infinite ways to botch it, so even though adolescence is technically the time when we are "supposed" to be doing the work of figuring out who we are and what we like, there are enormous swaths of us doing it in all decades of life. And we're often doing it not just once but over and over again as the conditions of our lives change, and with them, our wants and needs. Sometimes, learning to make a good wish is the work.

Ten of Cups

I n self-help book publishing every book has to have a "hook," which is a promise of what the book will do for the reader. The promise has to encapsulate both a problem and a solution. This is how creating products for mass consumption works. You convince people that there is a problem in their lives, and then tell them that you're offering the solution.

One of the biggest and most problematic "promises" I've come across in my years of writing in the fields of psychology and behavior is the promise of sustained happiness, which is a solution to the "problem" of basically any other emotion that isn't happiness. The premise here is that being happy is the goal of life, which makes a huge amount of sense from a marketing standpoint because if we can get people to believe that the goal of life is to feel good all the time, we can capitalize on the enduring reality that people will always have times of sadness, anxiety, jealousy, and dissatisfaction as long as they are alive. If we position that as a problem, we can sell endless products that promise to solve it. It's easy to sell products that promise happiness, but it also sets people up to feel like failures. So they keep buying stuff, hoping that this time it'll fix the "problem." But the gag is that the problem of having human emotions is unsolvable.

If you believe that happiness is the goal of life, the implication then is that sadness is failure. When a low or difficult emotional state gets framed as a "problem" to be solved, rather than as a natural and healthy part of the life experience—part of an inescapable ebb-and-flow rhythm to which we all belong—we've rejected a whole half of what life is. And then we wonder why we find ourselves stuck and in such trouble.

In 2017, positive psychology researchers published findings that suggested emodiversity—which they defined as "the breadth and relative abundance of emotions that individuals experience"—is more significant to wellness than happiness. When they asked 175 adults between the ages of forty and fifty to record their positive and negative emotions over thirty days, they discovered that those who reported a broader range of emotions had less inflammation, a biological process that has been linked to both early morbidity and mortality, but also to emotional states.

The Ten of Cups is one of the most interesting cards in the deck. Folk interpretations often say it's about living "happily ever after," or attaining a goal. But it's also a "stage" card, which means the characters are standing on what looks like a stage. This suggests that things may not be exactly as they seem. There is a family here, holding hands, dancing and giving a very convincing performance of joy. But the rainbow of cups in the sky tells a different story, that there is variation in the emotional energy of the card. In real life, the type of connection depicted here—family, intimacy, togetherness—is not all rainbows and butterflies. It's also anxiety, loss, envy, disappointment, fear, anger, despair. If it weren't so, why would there be a multicolored rainbow? Why not just a bright yellow stripe in the sky?

It makes sense that emodiversity would be an indicator of well-being. The more variations of emotion we're able and willing to feel, the freer we are because we rely less on rigid avoidance strategies to feel safe. Generally, people who have things they're absolutely not willing to feel are more likely to box themselves into behavioral corners. But barricading yourself off from the feelings you're scared of incurs a hefty cost. For example, if you structure your life around avoiding anxiety in social situations, the price you pay is your access to human connection. If you organize your life to avoid the uncertainty that comes with making a big change, the cost is extended and sustained feelings of indolence. Imagine trying to look at a rainbow and not wanting to see the color green. You'd have to close your eyes entirely, so you miss out on the rest.

Positive psychology sounds like it would be the "love and light" branch of psychology, but actually it encompasses love, hate, joy, sorrow, and everything in between. Positive psychologists have recognized that while the field has gotten pretty good at bringing people up from low moods and maladaptive behaviors to healthier baselines, it's been far less effective in helping people go beyond that baseline, from being okay to thriving. So in recent years, their research has focused more on understanding how the contrast between so-called positive and negative aspects of the human experience is misguided. And rather than divide experiences into positive and negative, the emphasis has been on the totality of well-being. Which includes the broad range of what we experience as positive and negative, good and bad— the stuff of a vital life.

Page of Cups

I n the Internal Family Systems model of psychotherapy, every person is considered to be a conglomeration of multiple parts. Within each of us lives a diverse inner community of various ages, memories, drives, and temperaments. The part of us that holds the traumas from childhood, according to this model, is often very young. This part has old coping strategies and beliefs that we are often unaware of until, usually through a process of healing work, we identify the times and places in which this part shows up, and we begin to get to know it.

There are several ways to think about the pages in tarot, but one of my favorite ways is to consider them as representing young members of an internal family. The Page of Cups lends itself well to this way of understanding because of their traditional symbolic qualities of innocence and sensitivity. Arthur Waite wrote that the Page of Cups is fair and young, "impelled to service... a studious youth" and that in a reading they often stand for "news, message; application, reflection, meditation." Rachel Pollack wrote that the fish can symbolize "psychic talents and sensitivity" and that this page represents "a time in which contemplation and fantasy are very proper to a person."

I consider the Page of Cups to carry the energy of a sensitive child. Which is to say, in a harsh world, that they are the "too-sensitive" child. Having been told many times that they were too sensitive throughout their youth, this is a psychological part of an adult who may find certain emotions to be unacceptable and unbearable. Natural feelings of sadness, loneliness, and fear are coupled and entwined with shame, having internalized reprimands like *Don't be such a crybaby. Relax. You're being too sensitive.*

Sadness, loneliness, and fear are hard enough on their own without shame braided in. But shame is a powerful motivator of behavior that can stimulate an intense urge to push away and avoid whatever other emotions it came with. Often that's done through actions that ultimately make life more painful.

If this sounds like you, first of all, you aren't too sensitive. It is totally possible to go back and uncouple an emotion from shame so that it feels less intense when it comes up in the present. You do this by making a space, whether alone or in the presence of a trusted other (such as a friend, partner, or therapist), to process that original feeling. The sadness, the loneliness, the fear. You were never wrong for feeling those things.

You needed validation and a space to feel, but what you got was punishment and ridicule. Recalling Waite's interpretation of the Page of Cups as a bearer of good tidings, the good news is that it isn't too late. You can get the validation you need now and make a space for all of your feelings. Validation and making space are at the heart of much therapeutic work. Tarot cards are a doorway, and this page is a portal back to a time of sensitivity and tenderness, where we might make right what was wrong.

Knight of Cups

owe so much of the way I understand people and relationships to the hundreds of behavioral science books I've had access to over my years in publishing. While I know there are experiences that can't and probably shouldn't be drilled down to a science, I'm always curious about scientific theories on things like love and romance. In one book, *ACT & RFT in Relationships*, a group of behavioral scientists attempt to understand romantic relationships through the studies of language and behavior. A lofty quest, but nonetheless noble.

According to the authors JoAnne Dahl, Ian Stewart, Christopher Martell, and Jonathan Kaplan, people in relationships set themselves up for failure when they think about love as an emotional state (which we're conditioned to do through things like fairy tales and rom-coms), particularly as one that's supposed to always feel good. Interested in the behavioral components of love, the authors note that viewing emotions as automatic determinants of behavior is always problematic because feelings are prone to rapid and sometimes extreme fluctuation. They write, "Sometimes people can feel what seems like 'true love,' while at other times they might not be sure; after a big argument, people can feel anger and even hatred toward each other.... Allowing emotion to dominate behavior—has the potential to make human relationships very unstable."

Because the reality of love, and any kind of close relationship, is that it hurts sometimes. When we feel anger or even hatred toward a partner, does that mean we've stopped loving them? Of course not.

The belief in love as a feeling can ruin relationships. It reduces a complex connection to a one-dimensional thing that owes us constant pleasure and joy. It makes love self-centered, rather than transcendent, an experience of something that brings us outside the lonely limits of our selves. The transformative power of love is tucked inside its ability to bring us into communion with something bigger and maybe more true than what we understand as our individual selves. It is *not* in some fantasy that love equals feeling good all the time. So the authors define love not as a feeling, but as a set of behaviors.

All of the knights in the Rider-Waite-Smith tarot deck are on horseback, which symbolizes action, behavior, that which one can be seen doing. The Knight of Cups deals specifically with the realm of water, a connecting energy that commonly manifests in human relationships. The idea of love as a set of actions works because it makes space for love to be something that can feel a lot of different ways— painful and stressful and boring at times—but we commit anyway. Instead of wondering what real love should feel like, we might ask, When I'm loving, what does it look like? When love is seen as a set of actions rather than a singular feeling, it becomes a safe container for uncomfortable emotions to come up in service of healing. Then love becomes a force for human evolution.

What's also brilliant about this idea of love as a set of behaviors is that you can apply it to self-love, too. Self-love can seem hard when we don't feel particularly affectionate toward ourselves. But if love is a set of actions, self-love doesn't need to be a prerequisite but can instead be a by-product of loving action. Of making choices rooted in self-preservation, honoring personal limits, and accommodating vulnerabilities with an eye toward the things that are precious. We can perform loving actions for others and ourselves, and let feelings come and go.

Queen of Cups

A primary task in all healing relationships—such as that between a therapist and client—is to listen deeply. Conversely, traumatic relationships are ones in which people consistently deny, overlook, and avoid each other's truths. Our imaginations make it easy to project fantasies about who another person is or ought to be rather than pausing to cultivate the willingness and psychological fortitude to be present with who they are truly, where they're at, and what they're available to offer in a relationship.

I think one of the things that makes it so easy for relationships to become traumatic is that it can be really hard to accept the truth of where people are at. We often think of the present moment as this inherently good, sort of idyllic place, but the reality is that without our fantasies to take the edge off, reality can be pretty painful and terrifying. When we're looking at someone through the foggy lens of what we'd hoped they could be or interpreting the way they're showing up as somehow having to do with us—a reflection of our unlovability or unworthiness—we're not doing deep listening. And deep listening is where healing becomes possible.

The Queen of Cups sits on the edge of the sea, not immersed in water but in intimate relationship with it, still. She holds a large chalice, perhaps symbolizing the emotional matter of others, which she holds lightly in her hands but with deep care. The chalice sits at a safe and appropriate distance from her body, her heart—perhaps symbolizing her own emotional field. She has a strong sense of which emotions are her work to sort through and which are for others, and she

229

understands how to act in alignment with that knowledge. She is an image of what's called exquisite empathy in the healthcare profession, which Richard Lawrence Harrison defined as "highly present, sensitively attuned, well boundaried, heartfelt empathic engagement."

I first learned of exquisite empathy as a graduate student seeking ways to cope with the overwhelming grief and anguish I was bearing witness to as an intern at a community mental health agency in an under-resourced community. It was during that time that I also learned about a thing called the "righting reflex," which is the compulsion to swoop in and attempt to "fix" people's problems for them. It didn't take long for me to realize that this urge was rooted in a somewhat delusional and problematic belief that it was my job to "fix" anything.

When I paused to examine what was underlying the righting reflex, I saw how little it had to do with the desire to provide the right medicine and how much it had to do with the need to distance myself from my own feelings of discomfort in the presence of others' suffering. Acting on the compulsion to make suffering go away—understandable and deeply human as it may be—is also a way of saying no to the present moment and making deep listening an impossible task. It is less about healing and restoration and more about distraction and avoidance. When it comes to emotional suffering—be it our own or the suffering of others—presence is typically the very first medicine that's needed. And to the extent that we're unable to be present with our own stuff, we're ill-equipped to attend appropriately to the stuff of others.

In her book *Waiting for God*, French philosopher Simone Weil writes that "the capacity to give one's attention to a sufferer is a very rare and difficult thing; it is almost a miracle; it is a miracle." In the legend of the Grail, she continues, the sacred treasure would be given to the first knight who arrived and asked the wounded king guarding the Grail, "What ails you?" Importantly, this one simple question was enough to heal the king and gain access to the treasure. No fix or solution was necessary.

King of Cups

An intellectualizer by both nature and nurture, I've often been confounded by the cups, the domain of water. They lack precision, defy logic, slide through the fingers. Delineations don't seem to work in the same way they do in the other suits. The cups are slippery and confusing. It can feel as if there are no boundaries. Nothing to hold on to.

Understanding in this domain requires raw feeling and direct experience, which it seems can only be accessed on a sort of subterranean level below the verbal and reasoning mind. To understand water means to give oneself over to its currents, instead of trying to put it into containers with the labels we might use to tell stories or make art. What we're asked to do here reminds me a bit of a scene in *Titanic*, when the lower levels of the ship are filling with water and Jack, seeking Rose, descends a staircase onto a flooded floor. He drops into the waves, goes from walking to swimming. That's what dealing with the cups domain feels like. You can talk and suppose and consider for years, and at a certain point you have to just drop in. So, in advance, forgive me if this gets a bit brackish.

The way that emotion and imagination move defies all physical boundaries in the realm of space and time. The way that we feel and imagine can move from an *intrapersonal*, private experience to an *interpersonal* experience occurring between two or more people instantly and invisibly. Grief and rage can transcend spatial, chronological, energetic, or psychic boundaries, moving from one body to another both horizontally—between individuals in the present day—and vertically, between people across generations. If you grew up in the nineties like I did, you might remember the Nickelodeon character Alex Mack, who had the power to turn into a mercurial liquid whenever she wanted, move fluidly and often imperceptibly to others between rooms and spaces. Emotions are kind of like that.

Emotions and imagination transcend what we consider to be personal limitations in that they're experienced both individually and collectively. A feeling or fantasy can be private, but can also be shared between two people, a group, or a family. People in cultures all over the world in geographic isolation from one another have generated and told stories with motifs and characters that echo or resemble one another since time out of mind. You will experience some emotions and you won't know where they came from. You won't be able to intellectually trace back the origins, and I don't think you necessarily need to.

Queens belong to the realm of imagination while kings belong to the domain of will. But for the King of Cups—King of Imagination—will looks different. Rather than find expression through physical exertion as we might think about with something like willpower, for example, the King of Cups has to do with willingness, a more receptive application of the will. Floating on the sea, he exists in a state of being prepared and ready to do what is required in order to accept and stay afloat as the waters rise. It is an active acquiescence.

A king might stand for one with the competence to find resolution where others had been unable to. Emotions are often passed down through generations until they reach someone who has the right set of resources and abilities to resolve them. Which is to say, to clear a space for them to emerge, unfold, and find full expression. Water has for so long been a symbol of birth and life, and I would argue that emotions, which are also associated with water, simply want what all other life wants: to be born, to have a safe space to express fully, and to die, eventually, as all living things do. While our human impulse is often to deny our feelings that fundamental right, the King of Cups protects it.

Emotions are like water, too, in that they can be powerful and all-consuming. They can "flood" us in just the same way that water can. When an emotion arises, which often happens rapidly, we can lose

234

our connection with the earth and have to make a deliberate effort to ground. One of my favorite ways to think about the King of Cups actually comes from Aleister Crowley's interpretation of the Knight of Cups,* which says that the character is "quick to respond to attraction and easily becomes enthusiastic under such stimulus, but he is not very enduring.... His name is writ in water." Emotions are like that, too. Quick to arouse, incredibly convincing in a moment of stimulation, but rarely in it for the long haul. To say that something is written in water is to say that it has a short shelf life, to say the least.

To be masterful in the emotional realm means to understand the life cycle of emotions. Here's a charm that's helped me internalize that understanding: Trauma expert Bessel van der Kolk has written that humans can endure more pain when they know it is time limited, which means that intellectually knowing the transient nature of emotions is a tool that helps us with the necessary task of experiencing it. This is how an emotion makes its way out of an individual, out of a family, and ultimately out of a bloodline. And so if you are feeling something big and deep, consider your kingship. Consider that maybe you are the one with the tools and the temperament to contain the thing and see it through, once and for all.

---

*The Thoth deck does not contain a king, and though the knight and king are probably not interchangeable, the symbol of the masculine in the water domain feels applicable.

Ace of Pentacles

When you're born you're given your own little plot of earth—a body—and with it the capacity to behave. Over time, you learn that no matter what may be happening for you internally—whatever thoughts and feelings you're experiencing—you have at least some degree of choice in the way you physically respond. The pentacles remind us of the necessity and power of understanding the sphere of influence that we do have: our behavior and what we physically choose to do in the world.

In my interpretations of tarot I associate the pentacles with behavior, because they're connected with the earth element and because the body—the vehicle with which we behave—is the one domain of the four that is material.

The coin is also a symbol of value. Its link with the behavioral domain strongly suggests that the things we hold precious are expressed through what we physically do. Said another way, what we care about is communicated in how we move through the world. This doesn't mean our choices don't at times betray what's precious to us. They do. In those moments, there may be a stronger, louder part of us for whom feeling safe or avoiding discomfort is most valuable. As a whole, the pentacles suit is an exploration of what we need to determine what's precious to us, and to act accordingly.

The hand that emerges from the sky in each of the aces in tarot echoes the motif of the "supernatural aid" in old stories. A magical or pseudomagical being appears on the path to give the hero a charm that will help them when they most need it. The charm here—the knowledge that is going to save you—is that while behavior is easily influenced by the other domains—thoughts, feelings, and energy—it doesn't have to be. With practice, you can cultivate a degree of behavioral sovereignty, or what's called psychological flexibility in the science of behavior. You can develop the ability to move in alignment with your values, no matter what your mind is doing.

This particular charm comes with some footnotes that I think will also aid you. First, behavior is defined as that which you can be seen doing. So if I have a thought that I'm hungry, that's not a behavior. But if I cook something to eat, that is. Second, behavior can, but is not required to, defer to and even take orders from the other domains, like thoughts and feelings.

The hunger example illustrates how the interplay between subtle, internal events—thoughts, feelings, and energy—and dense behavioral ones *can* lead to nourishment. Our thoughts exclaim, "I'm hungry!" and the body responds by preparing a delicious meal.

Where we get into trouble is when we indiscriminately do *everything* our thoughts, feelings, and energy tell us to do. Here's a quick example of how this interplay can work against you. Let's say you were invited to a party and your mind generates a thought like "I might say something stupid." That thought also has an implicit instruction tucked inside: "Stay home." You practice behavioral sovereignty—or psychological flexibility—when you recognize that you still have a choice to go or not go. And you practice behavioral sovereignty when, if it's in line with your values to go to the party, you go.

Another good thing to know is that just as internal events can stimulate behavior, the opposite can also be true; you can use behavior to affect how you feel. You won't always feel like doing the thing that you know is best for you—for instance, going for that walk, calling a good friend, getting out of bed—but you can do the thing anyway. And pay attention to how it affects your energy, feelings, or thoughts.

Folk interpretations of the pentacles suit often say that the coins have to do with career and finance, but I think these symbolize deeper human values of belonging and security. Seen this way, true security might come through knowing that you are—to a certain extent—in control of what you do and don't do no matter what your mind is telling you. That you can think and feel something without acting on it. That you can decide for yourself what is precious and move in accordance with that knowledge no matter what thoughts or feelings you may have in a given moment.

If belonging relates to a sense of community, and a community is a congregation of beings with shared values, then the capacity to determine our values and stay the course with them is what writer Toko-pa Turner calls a "competency of belonging." A sense that we are participating as cocreators of something greater than the individual, participating in what Hermeticists call "the great work of creation." That participation is, in my view, what the pentacles suit is all about.

Two of Pentacles

y friends and I often joke about the concept of fun. We wonder what it is exactly, how challenging it can be to actually have it, and why fun seems to come so easily to some, while others—for example, us—find it hard to detach long enough from the more troubled dimensions of life to enjoy themselves. So much of healing work is concerned with the prickly and painful things, the stuff that keeps us stuck in outdated patterns and structures, but just as joy without grief is merely half a life picture, the same is true for too much time spent in the somber without any fun or laughter mixed in.

On the quest to better understand fun, I did what anyone with a tendency to engage life through the intellect would do: a bit of reading. Which is where I came across the work of psychiatrist Shimi Kang. In an interview, Kang talked about how our brains have feedback loops that give us information about how to create balance in our lives. When we get hungry, we eat. When we're tired, we sleep. When we feel lonely, we call a friend. But in modern life, we've become so disconnected from these feedback loops that a lot of us don't even realize we feel bad because we haven't slept, or because we're not eating enough, or because we're not doing the things that nourish our minds and bodies. We've gotten so good at analyzing and psychologizing that we've forgotten how to listen to the simple sounds of what our bodies are saying. A lot of the time we don't even know we're *supposed* to be listening.

Maybe our ancestors didn't need to know they were supposed to be listening, either, they just did because their survival depended on it.

The conveniences of modern life make it so that we don't really have to listen, or at least we don't feel like we have to—that is, until we're sick, burnt out, or depleted. In reading Kang's work I realized that balance isn't just about the basics like eating and sleeping. It's also about having fun and being playful. Especially for those who spend a disproportionate amount of time engaging with hard, serious things.

Donald Winnicott, who was a pioneer in the field of child development, described play as a process in which a paradox had "to be accepted, tolerated, and not resolved." He felt that play required people to switch off the brain's instinct toward caution. And this makes intuitive sense because play requires the deployment of imagination to experience a reality that lives somewhere between the material and the imagined. In a world as desperately in need of people with the capacity to dream new realities as ours is, this strikes me as a crucial life skill.

Kang said that play activates the brain's prefrontal cortex and helps us learn to settle into spaces of unpredictability. The coins in the Two of Pentacles are airborne but could fall at any time; they exist in a constant state of movement as represented by the infinity sign that wraps around and holds them together. This is a genius visual representation of what happens when we play, I think. Play is vital, says Kang, because "without it we have difficulty developing new ideas and concepts. We become perfectionists who can't make mistakes because we are uncomfortable with it."

It's easy to see how there might be a link between rule-laden perfectionism and reluctance or difficulty engaging in play. Those of us who run our lives like tight ships leave little space for unpredictability. This unpredictability is what makes fun different from something like the pleasure that comes with eating a meal you know is going to be fantastic or discussing something you're passionate about with a good friend who shares your enthusiasm. Those things contain within them a controlled kind of pleasure, which isn't to say they're not important, just that they may not have the same medicinal quality for the person with an overly serious life who knows they need fun but struggles to tolerate the uncertainty of play.

A couple of weeks before writing this I went sledding with a six-year-old in a foot of fresh snow and we slid so slowly down the hill we had to use our arms to get to the bottom. That was fun. I think what made it fun was that it wasn't what I expected, so there was an element of surprise and of not being in control, but it wasn't scary or dangerous. Maybe play is when you give yourself over to situations where your ideas about what things are and how they will go can get disrupted in a way that's delightful and safe. Maybe in that process you learn that it's safe to make mistakes in other areas of life, too. Maybe.

Three of Pentacles

monk, an architect, and a sculptor meet up inside a building. They're doing a project together, it seems. Within their individual areas of expertise, it's safe to assume that they each have strengths and limitations. The boundaries that exist between them—what they each can and cannot do—is, as all boundaries are, both the thing that differentiates them and the point where they converge. In this place of confluence appears a portal.

Critical theorist Homi Bhabha pioneered the term *hybridity* in the context of cultural identity, which he defines as "a doubling, dissembling image of being in at least two places at once." Emerging from hybridity is a third space, "something different, something new and unrecognizable, a new area of negotiation of meaning and representation." In the Three of Pentacles, three people with three distinct identities walk into a shared space, suggesting that something is created in the coming together of their unique contributions.

The image asks us to consider that as much as a boundary is a limit, it's also a meeting place. A place where we identify and name what we can and cannot bring, and where we locate our edges in relationships with others. That edge, where personal limits are seen and accounted for, makes way for the emergence of something that is uniquely possible in that particular confluence of energies.

There are boundaries within each of us where different parts of us come together, too. Carl Jung talked about *transcendent function*, which feels related to Bhabha's hybridity. Transcendent function has to do with understanding and finding value in what can emerge when conflicting parts within us meet and clash. Perhaps when a person is torn between obligation and desire, for instance, something new can emerge, a third thing that braids together what we should do and what we want to do. In making a space for that tension, what once felt like a hard knot may begin to loosen a bit.

In another interpretation of the Three of Pentacles—and I think incorporating a number of perspectives is in keeping with this card's secrets—the architect might represent a logical part of the mind, loyal to physical evidence and data, what's called "reasonable mind" in dialectical behavior therapy (DBT). The sculptor may symbolize what DBT calls "emotion mind," an imaginative part of the mind that draws more on what's felt and invisible to make choices. When a person is receiving directives from both reasonable mind and emotional mind, a third way can appear, a middle passage between the two directives, called "wise mind." Maybe that's what the monk stands for.

One of the reasons I find Jung's work interesting is his use of alchemical language to describe psychological experiences. He said that the "solvent," or the agent that can blend two seeming opposites, occurs not through logic alone or emotion alone but through an energetic process "just as a waterfall visibly mediates between above and below." The combination of two things creates something else entirely. Sometimes we have to be the vessel that holds the two things patiently, waiting for that precious third thing to emerge.

Space needs to be made not only for what we think and what we feel—and what others think and feel—but also for the stuff that arises in the spaces where these different energies conflict. It is in holding this tension that Jung says "a third thing in which opposites can unite" emerges.

Four of Pentacles

've had a committed almost-daily yoga practice for years, and it's given me many things, but by far one of the most useful has been the opportunity to practice transcending and accepting limitations, or blocks, through the physical body.

In the early days of my practice, I studied with a teacher named Peter Sanson, who compared doing a yoga pose to creating a circuit with the body. He taught that through focused use of the breath and gaze, a practitioner can move energy through the pose or circuit, increasingly moving that energy into stuck spaces. He was very clear that doing it this way requires gentle curiosity, and not force.

In my own experience, I can see how force seems to exacerbate blocks—often manifesting as injury—while gentle curiosity is often more effective in slowly melting away or clearing blocks altogether.

There is a strong and automatic tendency to respond to stuckness with hostility and aggression. So many times, teachers have asked me, "Why are you forcing?" and it's taken a lot of practice to remind myself that no one's keeping time. No one is grading me on my ability to make a particular shape with my body, or to respond differently to a trigger, or to do a new thing that I'm scared of, for that matter.

When I teach people to read tarot in the way that I practice, I fold in a lot of ideas from the tradition of narrative therapy, a natural fit since tarot card reading is in many ways a storytelling practice. Approaching our challenges through narrative is one way to sort of hack the intellectual mind in order to change the way we relate to our problems, or "blocks," through reframing and perspective shifting. When we relate differently to something, we tend to behave differently around it. As social worker Mary Van Hook has written, "Stories don't mirror life, they shape it."

Like so: the fact that you've even identified something as a block means movement is happening. When you hit a wall, that's literally only happening because you're trying to move energy in a different direction, walk through a new doorway, or dig a new tunnel. And sometimes you have to jiggle the handle a little or learn how to use a different tool because there's something new in the way. Calling something a "block," "limit," or "challenge" is a protest in itself, a statement or declaration that you're not okay with being constrained in this particular way, and you most certainly do *not* plan to shape a life around some limitation that really doesn't need to be there.

The Four of Pentacles just looks like the word *block* to me. Pentacles cover the crown of the head, blocking awareness; the heart, blocking connection and understanding; and the soles of the feet, blocking action. Because a pentacle is a physical thing, it makes me think of practices like asana, one of the physical components of yoga, which is one of many paths of spiritual work through the physical body. Doing postures with a body that has limitations and areas of stuckness is one way of exploring which attitudes and narratives are most effective for clearing blocks, as well as for learning to live better with them.

With any kind of block, the first task is to be present enough to notice that it is there—whether it be physical, behavioral, energetic, emotional, or psychological—rather than either avoiding it altogether or trying to muscle through it. Avoidance and forcefulness both seem to have a tendency to make blocks worse, the former by reinforcing a belief that the block is dangerous to make contact with, and the latter by piling on more energy rather than patiently working to clear the existing backlog. Maybe we could remind ourselves that it isn't dangerous to investigate blocks, but that we can always do so gently, giving ourselves full permission to back off anytime it gets to feel like too much.

And I think noticing a block is in itself something to celebrate. You might not think so, those around you might not think so, but I think it is, because it's when you know you're ready to do the work. Identifying a block means you get to start poking around to find the malleable parts, the parts with some give, where transformation could happen, little by little. As you go, you'll learn what qualities of mind are best when working with these things. Some that I've found helpful when engaging with blocks are gentleness, curiosity, humor, and patience. You'll see what works for you.

Five of Pentacles

ne of my favorite quotes ever is by travel writer Pico Iyer, who writes, "Heaven is the place where you think of nowhere else." It always makes me wonder, if that's what heaven is, maybe hell is the place where you have everything you've ever wanted but you can't access it; you can't stop thinking about something else, someone else, somewhere else.

Joseph Campbell talked about eternity as not a matter of infinite linear time but rather a dimension where "all thinking in temporal terms cuts off." He said, "Eternity isn't some later time. Eternity isn't even a long time. Eternity has nothing to do with time.... And if you don't get it here, you won't get it anywhere." I take this to mean that eternity is an experience of accessing the present moment.

I don't know about you, but 99 percent of the time when I hear someone say the words *present moment*, my eyes glaze over. It feels trite and poorly seen through. There's no immediate promise or inherent value associated with being present, and I've often wondered why I or anyone would want to leave a safely dissociated fantasy world in favor of a place that can be so painful, heavy, and terrifying.

So first, let's all just acknowledge that the present moment is not some utopian village before we start inviting people here en masse on false pretenses. The present isn't always an easy place to be; it takes skills to be here. Skills that, like all abilities, require practice and usually some unlearning. But here's why this matters, why it's worth doing: The ability to be present is a prerequisite for feeling fulfilled. And if you can't do it here, you won't be able to do it anywhere. If one day, you woke up and all your dreams had come true, without the capacity to be present, you would be just as ill-equipped to enjoy those things as you were before you had them.

The Five of Pentacles is one of the secrets in tarot that doesn't require much finessing to be told. It activates a lot right away, has no problem being vulnerable with strangers. It whispers things about being sad, lonely, left out, abandoned, and destitute. Its voice cracks around a lump in its throat as it speaks openly of hardship. I think what makes it so sad is that the warmth and connection that the wanderers so visibly need is immediately available to them—we can practically see the hugs, blankets, and tender meats falling off the bone through the glow of the windows—but they can't or aren't sure how to get inside. One looks to the right, one straight ahead, but neither looks directly toward the thing they need most.

Sadly, this is an experience many of us can relate to. You get the job, partner, or home you've always wanted and it feels good for a while but somehow it still, ultimately, doesn't quite cut it. Soon enough you're browsing job ads, questioning whether you're with the right person— sometimes to the point of obsession—and perusing apartment listings in other cities when you're bored. Accessing your blessings is as much a psychological capacity as it is a physical one, and perhaps that's why the wealthiest people in the world are bottomless pits that devour obsessively as the world around them starves.

In the language of symbol, coldness—winter, snow, ice—stands for a lack or loss of feeling. This gives a hint about why we can struggle so much to be in the present and illuminates a trail that goes toward knowing how to access both its charms and challenges.

We first learn to leave the present as a way to numb or protect ourselves from things we don't know how to cope with otherwise. But while leaving in this way can protect us from things we want to avoid, it also prevents us from connecting with things that are good for us. In the somatic Hakomi method of psychotherapy, this leaving is called a nourishment barrier, a self-erected psychic force field that blocks us from absorbing the nutritive elements in the things we experience, like intimacy, caring relationships, or success in whatever that means to us.

Sometimes this barrier manifests as compulsively scheming about the future, rumination on the past, or endless efforts to control how others think, feel, and act to distract from our own thoughts, feelings, and behaviors. Sometimes it looks like numbing out entirely, which unsurprisingly is referred to as "freezing" in certain fields of medical practice.

These trapdoors and exit strategies helped us survive a long time ago. We didn't have better ways to be safe then, but we do now. We do not need to stay there, frozen in our personal antiquities, doomed to eat old, rotting food that once kept us alive but is bordering on poison at this point. We do not need to eat rancid food or take expired medicines when there are fresh foods here in the present. There are potent, fast-acting elixirs with almost no side effects. Delicious fruits and fragrant blossoms and the warmest hugs. And I'm not going to lie to you, there is bitter taste, too. There are pungent, nasty smells and excruciating losses here. But you have what you need to cope with those. It'll take practice, and ultimately you'll need to see for yourself, but it is safe for you to be here.

Six of Pentacles

Being in the social work field has made me think a lot about hierarchies, particularly those that are built on the binary of the well and the unwell. I came into social work looking through the lens of functional contextualism, a philosophy that's used to understand behavior as always serving a function in a given context. It didn't take long for me to notice that I felt an almost magnetic pull toward being in a role of healer, helper, or teacher in relationships, both professional and personal. And it felt imperative to the well-being of all involved that I unpack why that was so, what I was getting out of being in that role, and what function it served for me.

What this inquiry has helped me to understand is that when we erect hierarchies in any type of relationship—whether that be the therapist who maintains a position of power by disclosing nothing about themselves, or the partner who is constantly trying to "help" the other without ever asking for what they themselves need—we are investing in a structure that unevenly distributes things like care, resources, vulnerability, and, as a result, power. When all the care or attention is being funneled toward one person, the caregiver is blocked from being seen or known. And I think that's often rooted in an unconscious aversion to being seen, a deep-seated fear that intimacy is dangerous, and a sense that the things we need and want will betray us or reveal the ways in which we are too much, not enough, or downright broken. This is what I see when I look at the Six of Pentacles, and I can't unsee it.

I haven't worked as a therapist outside of my training in graduate school, but I have spent years studying psychotherapies and participating in the therapeutic process as a client. One of the things that makes the relationship between a therapist and client so fascinating is that its primary function is healing, which means there's much everyday people can glean from the research that's been done about what makes for a restorative relationship and what makes for a destructive one. Psychoanalyst Izette de Forest wrote that analysts who shy away from really using themselves in their work—allowing their own emotions to come up and be a part of the therapeutic process—were afraid of their own "impulses... weakness... lack of self-knowledge," and that while staying rooted in the role of teacher allowed a therapist to maintain a persona of strength and wisdom, it was based in a fundamental anxiety and insecurity, and fostered a kind of dependence on the therapist that was not ultimately in the patient's best interest. I'd argue that in our personal relationships, when we peek under the hood of our compulsive giving and caretaking, we may well find that the compulsion to give as though we are bottomless belies deep fears of abandonment. In making ourselves indispensable to someone, we might fool our hearts into believing that the person will never leave, or we divert attention from our own neuroses, which we fear are grounds for rejection.

The person in the Six of Pentacles who gives coins to those begging does so in a measured way, so mechanically that it's impossible to see the complex messiness of who he is (as we all are) in the process, and it feels likely to me that he prefers it that way. Those begging, on the other hand, practically bare their souls—palms out, faces to the sky in a posture of utter vulnerability. Further, in giving *coins*—rather than something of real and enduring value, like letting oneself be moved through deep listening or sharing direct access to an ongoing source of provisions—the quality and impact of this relationship is deeply questionable.

When we don't let ourselves be known, we make ourselves untouchable by those we care for. But it is two-way, dynamic, heart-to-heart touch that makes deep healing possible. After all, it was in deep connection that our oldest injuries were sustained, and so perhaps it is in deep connection that the roots of such wounds might be properly treated.

Seven of Pentacles

I used to interpret the Seven of Pentacles as a card about putting in work and seeing that work pay off. The feeling when you've poured blood, sweat, and tears into a project, and it yielded the results you wanted. But then I started working with Aleister Crowley and Lady Frieda Harris's Thoth tarot deck, and the word *failure* at the bottom of their Seven of Pentacles card had me puzzled. I've since learned that this sort of confusion can be a good thing. For those with ears to hear, it means you're about to get told a new secret.

The first time I heard the quote "you can never get enough of what you don't really need," I'd just finished graduate school. I remember feeling like I was supposed to be really excited and proud, but all I wanted to do was forget for a while and go see my friends in California. In old stories, there's a motif about difficult tasks where a protagonist has to separate thousands of poppy seeds from a dirt pile or slay a dragon and then sow its teeth like seeds in the ground to get treasure. Graduate school was a quest that involved many such difficult tasks, and as is the case with the completion of all hard jobs, there were big decisions to make afterward about what was truly precious, and how to move forward with that knowledge.

There's an old tale by Hans Christian Andersen in which a small girl in winter sells matches on the street for pennies. The matches themselves could help the girl build a fire that would warm her through the night, but she must sell them in order to return home. Despite her best efforts to trade something with life-sustaining value for something of far less value, she is unsuccessful and, eventually, perishes. In

261

another tale, a destitute mother heats stones on the stove for her children to suck on and make-believe are apples. Which reminds me a lot of the Seven of Pentacles. Here is a person who worked their hands to the bone, for what? A field of metal disks, items with no intrinsic or nutritive value. A crop they cannot chew, swallow, or digest. A true failure.

I bet we've all sucked on stones while pretending to be satiated. And if you've never sold off a life-giving thing in exchange for something that leaves you shivering, well, you're rare. These questions about true need, nourishment, and value are not trivial nor are they easy to answer. Partly because there are soul needs, and there are survival needs, and in the context of capitalism these things can—and very often do—conflict. To the point that figuring out what we truly require starts to feel a lot like sifting poppy seeds from the dirt.

The majority of us have done our own selves dirty through desperate, bad bargains and rushed, raw deals. We've traded attention and energy—our most precious and nonrenewable resources—for onetime use, disposable things with no real generative properties. But suck on stones as we may do, trade matches for pennies, we aren't fools. Even the worst deals we do in life served a purpose once, and if we want to do better, finding out more about what that purpose was may be helpful.

Maybe we were hoping to be rescued. Maybe we were scared of the feeling we'd get walking away. Maybe we took a wrong turn and knew it but weren't ready to give up the dream yet. Being truthful about what we need does begin with an earnest exploration of what that might be, but too often this comes only after having sold off valuables we'll never get back, and endured bellyaches from swallowing things that don't nourish us. And sure, we can call those things failures, but we can also call them a vital part of a process in which we learn to do the kinds of deals that bring us closer to what we require.

Eight of Pentacles

n acceptance and commitment therapy (ACT), clients are encouraged to identify their values and then determine what they're willing to accept—what they'd be willing to feel and experience internally—in order to make and keep a commitment to what they've deemed precious. Commitment is a core feature of ACT, obviously, and the process is unique in that it doesn't just ask for commitment but directly targets the reasons we struggle to keep the promises we make to ourselves.

The word *commitment* can feel like an obligation we make to others, and in fact that feeling is supported by the word's etymological roots. The Latin *committere* means "to unite, connect, combine" and "to bring together," while the fifteenth-century English use was to "consign (someone) to custody (of prison, a mental institution, etc.) by official warrant." But at the heart of ACT is the importance of connecting with our own notion of what is valuable, not what someone else has said we should want. So even when it does involve another person, a commitment is ultimately a deal you make with yourself.

Scholars of Western mysticism Caitlín Matthews and John Matthews write that "the techniques of the shaman, magician, and mystic are founded upon continuous practice and repeated effort informed by spiritual dedication and are focused by ethical intention.... [They] begin with such unglamorous practices as repetitive meditation, training the mind, honing perception, and searching the soul."

In the Eight of Pentacles, a craftsman sits alone at a workbench. He's closer to the edge of town than the village center, an indication of solitude and dedication. He's hammering away at a pentacle, which he's made and replicated numerous times, symbolizing the monotony of the "repetitive meditation" that mastery requires. The concept of repetition here may not be literal but rather metaphorical, representing the often mundane and unglamorous work that's needed to nourish the roots of new growth. Because "if we neglect the roots of the tree in order to reach for the fruit of the branches," write Matthews and Matthews, "we may find that the fruit has not set because the roots have not been nourished."

I don't think it's hard to make a case for sticking with commitments, but I do think the conversation is incomplete without an exploration of what often makes that so hard for people. Here are some of the things I've seen that make it tough to stay the course:

Fear of failure masquerading as apathy. This one's common for people who believe that failure is the worst thing that could happen and therefore is to be avoided at all costs. Symptoms may include internal narratives that sound something like "Why try, when I've tried one hundred times already and it didn't pan out?" Well, everything is always "panning out," meaning that it's evolving and devolving, arriving and leaving. It's just not always unfolding exactly in the way we want it to. Which leads us to the next reason.

Entitlement, and a sense that life owes you the results you want. Entitled people are those who, in the words of Jay-Z, tend to "emulate the end result and not the process." Preoccupied with fruits, they have little or no interest in the reality that the life cycle of fruit involves labor—the boring, exhausting, or tedious parts of the process—and feel unduly burdened by the thought of having to work for something. Because commitment almost always includes doing something when you don't feel like it, people who feel entitled to constant stimulation and pleasure often have a tough time, too.

Avoidance of aversive internal events is another one. Avoidant people make commitments that they quickly abandon upon realizing that moving forward is going to require they be willing to feel something they're scared of. Anxiety, grief, self-doubt, fear, inadequacy, boredom, you name it. A good commitment for an avoidant person might be to identify what they've historically been unwilling to feel, and then to build up the coping and distress-tolerance muscles to face those things. Because unfortunately, repeated abandonment of commitments often breeds apathy, and apathy makes a lot of things harder.

And then there's just bad aim. Sometimes the reason people can't commit is because the thing they've identified as precious means everything to someone else and nothing to them. Sometimes when you're continuously struggling to move toward a goal or vision, it's simply time to reevaluate how important that goal or vision really is to you. If your goal has no *real* value—for example, if it is aimed toward impressing others, scoring good reviews with imaginary critics, or proving your worthiness (which isn't up for debate to begin with)—that might explain why you're not making any progress.

The way toward what's precious begins with determining what's personally worth pursuing, and the journey is often long, arduous, and uncertain. It requires discipline, which is the way of one who takes apprenticeship to the commitment itself and thereby reaps the knowledge that blooms through that process. *Process* is a word we encounter over and over again in the pentacles suit. To quote Clarissa Pinkola Estés, "The work is to keep doing the work."

Nine of Pentacles

sometimes think of maturity as the ability to make good decisions on behalf of your future self. You understand that anything you plant, you'll harvest later, for better or for worse, and so you sow wisely, which sometimes means doing things you don't feel like doing or forgoing short-term gratification.

It's the mark of a wise person to know—having spent many a long, late night knee-deep in the mud of a bad deal—that it's not some other person who's going to have to dig you out. It is you. When you're mature you understand that the you of the future is the you of today. And perhaps most important, this "you" is someone you've gotten to know well enough to feel protective of, even when that's hard. The fact that this card comes so late in the suit is a reminder that, like all trusting relationships, this quality of connection with oneself requires time and patience.

The field of humanistic psychology emerged in the 1960s as a "third force" following the first force of psychoanalysis and the second force of behaviorism. One of the assumptions of humanistic approaches was that we all have a basic drive toward what Abraham Maslow called "self-actualization," or the realization of our gifts and potentials.

Ron Smothermon, a physician associated with the Human Potential Movement, which was born out of the humanistic psychology tradition, wrote, "No one is powerful enough to make you handle your life responsibly. You don't have to, and you are not even wrong if you don't. And there are consequences. And if you do choose to handle problems in your life responsibly, you won't even be right for doing it. And there will be consequences."

As an adult, you are the only one who ultimately decides whether you'll handle your life responsibly. No one's going to enforce that you do what you need to do today in order to be well later. No one's going to insist that you delay instant gratification for a long-term payoff, or that you do something hard in support of your own future peace and wellness. Everyone's too busy trying to secure these things for themselves. And the best part about all of this is that, honestly, you can do what you need to do, or not. It's totally on you.

One of the most important lessons of the pentacles suit as it connects to the domain of behavior is to recognize the areas in life in which we have power, and to learn to exert our energies in those areas in order to live our potential. To quote Lewis Hyde, "Each being in this world must find the set of opportunities fitted to its nature."

Most of the time we don't have control over the thoughts, emotions, or energetic drives we experience, but to at least some extent, we do have control over our behavior. When we've achieved a certain degree of skill in the realms of cognition, emotion, and energy, we find that we're more able to make good behavioral choices in the moment even when our thoughts, feelings, or urges tell us to do otherwise. It's interesting the way that the four domains of tarot build off one another, the way mastery in one realm supports growing proficiency in others. I think the gardens pictured throughout the pentacles suit in particular are a nod to the interdependent nature of the four domains, the way that energy, feelings, behavior, and thoughts interact and can either fortify and strengthen or create trouble for one another.

The woman in the Nine of Pentacles stands comfortable in a garden setting with a bird on her hand. There's an old story from the Sotho people from the southernmost region of Africa in which a hero frees all of humanity from the belly of a monster. At first, they make him their king, but soon after turn against him. Despite many efforts to get back in the people's good graces and escape their attempts on his life, the hero realizes there is nothing he can do to change their hearts and minds. He gives himself over to them, and when he dies, the story says that his heart turns to a bird and flies away.

The bird—in both the story and this card—stands for freedom. The protagonist becomes free only when he accepts that he cannot control others, only himself. I think the bird in the card stands for the particular type of liberation that comes with knowing that no matter what might be unfolding, we can choose to allow that which we have no control over—including our own unwanted thoughts and feelings—to arise. Our freedom lives in the acceptance that no matter what we might be thinking or how we may feel in a given moment, we can always make choices on behalf of our future selves.

Ten of Pentacles

I wrote the first draft of this book in a tiny tree house apartment that overlooked a botanical garden in the Berkeley Hills. Despite the fact that I'd been studying and writing about tarot for years by then—had even been tasked with writing a book about it—it was there that I first learned the concept of anima mundi, or world soul, which came to me by way of the writings of psychologist James Hillman.

The idea of a world soul is an old one—said to come from the ancient Greeks, though likely not unique to them—that expresses an intrinsic web of connection between all life. It suggests that rather than understanding psyche or soul as something that exists inside the confines of the individual human body, soul is woven through every living thing and is therefore something we all exist inside. I'm told this is a very old philosophy of psychology. That is, the study of the soul.

While I was writing this book, we went into lockdown due to the COVID-19 pandemic. With the privilege to stay mostly in isolation, I took to learning old stories from some of my ancestral homelands—namely southern Italy and Sardinia—and walking the hills of the East Bay, where I'd recite them aloud and imagine that the birds and trees were listening. For me, this seemed a practical way to facilitate a shift from the *anthropocentric*, or human-centered notion of soul, and toward something that more closely resembled a place inside the ecological anima mundi.

Looking at the Ten of Pentacles, it seems obvious that the card depicts an ecological notion of soul. The pentacles are arranged in the

273

shape of the Kabbalistic tree of life, a map of interconnected nodes defined by scholar of Jewish mysticism Eliezer Segal as "ten creative forces that intervene between the infinite, unknowable God... and our created world." On a practical level, the card's intergenerational and interspecies imagery—depicting people young and old, and humans and dogs—connotes interdependence, and suggests that all are connected and that *because* that is true, ideals like freedom and healing are inherently more than individual pursuits.

On the modern understanding of soul as existing inside each individual, psychologist Mary Watkins has written that "the hoarding of soul within interiority has served a defensive function, protecting us from the tragedies and travesties in our midst." Were we to throw ourselves from the tower of individualism and relinquish those protections, or, as Watkins puts it, "to break our attention free from its circumscription by purely personal pursuits, we will find ourselves feeling small, amidst many bits and pieces that do not seem to cohere," and importantly that "to accept a sense of being overwhelmed and inadequate to the situation is necessary."

The Ten of Pentacles seems to me the "lesser secret" that most closely corresponds to the greater secret of the World, one in which, having transcended the way of seeing in terms of pairs of opposites—self and other, individual and collective, internal and external—there is diversity, plurality, and the overwhelming experience of connection.

Hoarding soul inside interiority, we feel justified in also hoarding resources; we take more than we need to avoid the terrifying sense of being "small, amidst many bits and pieces that do not seem to cohere." We act out of self-interest rather than in the interest of the whole. Too afraid to relinquish our partitions, we relinquish our membership in community for an illusion of control. What, then, would it take for us to re-member ourselves? What would we need to be willing to feel in order to give up the life jacket of individualism and the idea that freedom for any single individual is adequate?

I am not close to having answers to these questions, but I do think there are secrets tucked into the pentacles suit, particularly as it relates to ideas about what we know is precious and acting in accordance with that knowledge. Not in a vague spiritual sense, but in a practical, material sense. In the words of cultural historian Thomas Berry, "We must say of the universe that it is a communion of subjects, not a collection of objects." The COVID-19 pandemic may be as close to a direct, collective initiation back into that re-membering as we are going to get. We are creatures inside a web, and our work is to develop a more ecological understanding of how our individual behavioral choices affect the world, and vice versa.

Page of Pentacles

he pentacles suit is connected with the Empress, who is commonly interpreted as a symbol of nature, fertility, and creation. In *The Book of Thoth*, Aleister Crowley writes that the Princess of Disks—who is not the same as Arthur Waite's Page of Pentacles but who does appear to share quite a few characteristics—"bears within her the secret of the future." Crowley continues, "She is strong and beautiful, with an expression of intense brooding, as if to become aware of secret wonder."

Lon Milo DuQuette, in his interpretations of the Thoth tarot, writes that the Princess of Disks, like Demeter, Greek goddess of harvest and fertility, "arises in her glory from out of the Earth itself and establishes her altar in the midst of a grove of barren and dying trees that her fertile presence will now restore to green health." A green altar erected in a forest of ailing trees. If there is a more potent, fertile, wild visual than that one, I'm not sure I've experienced it.

Learning new behaviors is a way of erecting a living altar in the areas of our lives that have become dry, stiff, or barren. The spaces where year after year crops fail or the harvest we'd hoped for doesn't come. The plots of land in our lives where what does manage to grow is weak, brittle, or diseased. The Page of Pentacles symbolizes the way in which such living altars—behavioral choices that sow the seeds of new norms, habits, and patterns—contain what Crowley called the "secret of the future." An altar always has to do with the temporal; it is a space on which to perform rituals that re-create myth and give life to the past. They are also spaces where we keep an eye toward the future, making faithful burnt offerings in exchange for something hoped for. Maybe the physical body is also an altar, a space in which we perform devotional acts with our behaviors as offerings.

The American Psychological Association defines pathology as "any departure from what is considered healthy or adaptive." This definition says that pathological behavior is the stuff we do that's compulsive, automatic, or seemingly beyond the locus of our control even when it yields damage. Behavior change is a way of setting up a kind of living altar that is not only in devotion to a new way of life but also in defiance of that within us which was previously automatic, unmagical, or unmiraculous. As we move through the pentacles suit, we gather up that which is necessary to build living altars with our behavior, as if that wisdom were a bouquet of wildflowers, offering lessons in clearing blocks, identifying what's precious, learning to commit, and gaining maturity.

The Page of Pentacles represents the emerging capability to use behavior in a way that is devotional. Once we know how to perform magic using the dense matter of our physical actions, we can do it anytime, anywhere, and in any way we choose. And then each new behavior becomes like an item placed on an altar. Carefully chosen, intentionally placed, with ties to the future and a harvest that is plentiful in the ways we hope for.

Knight of Pentacles

In the Stages of Change model, which was developed by psychologists James Prochaska and Carlo DiClemente, the action stage is the phase of change when a person has begun to actively use new behaviors. This stage occurs after someone has made a commitment to change based on an understanding of why that change will be beneficial, but the change isn't yet habitual, which is to say it still takes effort. This is a unique time in the process of making any kind of change, and it comes with unique challenges.

One of the most common difficulties in the action stage of change is the sense of not being totally on board with the change. Maybe you're trying to quit smoking, and you daydream of cigarettes on your lunch break. Or you're trying to minimize social media use, and you have to fight urges to check your phone multiple times an hour. A part of you is still set in the old way, is even fearful of a new way, and that's 100 percent normal.

It's normal to be behaviorally committed to a change—that is, moving in accordance with a decision to do something new—but having to do so while carrying some ambivalence. There's actually so much power in understanding this. It means you can experience urges, cravings, desires, yearnings, and also fears about letting an old way go, and still do what needs to be done. I've read the Knight of Pentacles described as "the builder"; the thing that's being built here, perhaps more than anything, is behavioral sovereignty, the ability to move in the direction of your choosing no matter what your thoughts, feelings, or sensations might be telling you.

The Knight of Pentacles has been described as not particularly intelligent, but I think that's a bit misleading. I think the meaning behind that statement is that this is a knight who does what needs to be done and doesn't think or feel too much about it. He represents the part in each of us that has the ability to override the constant fluctuations of the mind, like urges to revert to an old behavior or obsessive thoughts about something we're struggling to give up. He's depicted standing still—solid as a rock—symbolizing the steadiness of body that is required when so much is happening on the inside. It's not clear from the illustration, but I like to imagine that his mind might be screaming at him to turn back.

No matter what his mind might be saying or not saying, he holds firm. He can sit there as long as he needs to. And as he does he learns a secret: urges don't last that long. And even though urges early in the action stage might arise often and in rapid succession, the more he makes himself still and stays committed to where he wants to be, they do pass and eventually lessen in both frequency and intensity. In the process, though, he learns that he doesn't need to rely on the disappearance of urges because he's learned a new way of relating to them. He makes his body still and lets them pass. But it's also true that the less he takes orders from them, the less often they come. And so he keeps going.

And I know that keeping going is a lot easier said than done, especially when some part or parts of you are not on board with the change you're making, when there is terror, fury, foot stomping, and the gnashing of teeth. Counselors in the addiction recovery field often use something called motivational interviewing to support people in making big changes, in which they use questions to help people make connections between the new behaviors they're doing and the positive changes that are happening as a result. We can all do that for ourselves when we're doing something new and our minds and hearts are feeling scared, angry, or simply unsure about it.

When your mind is generating nonstop thoughts about something you truly want to let go of, you may feel as though you are powerless to stop it, and maybe you are. I can hear Joseph Campbell here saying,

"The mind can ramble off in strange ways and want things that the body does not want." In that case, your best bet might be to locate the points where you actually do have power, like in the things you physically do or don't do, no matter what your thoughts are doing. Sit on your hands. Be like a boulder, stone still for days if you have to. That's power.

Queen of Pentacles

I spent a lot of time sitting with the Queen of Pentacles in the summer of 2020, months into a pandemic with no end in sight and as protests erupted around the country in response to the murder of George Floyd by police officers.

It's interesting to see the role that social media plays in times when privileged people are faced with the possibility that who we believe ourselves to be and who we actually are in our day-to-day lives are at odds. It's hard to reconcile, for example, the fact that we live in a country where public health crises disproportionately impact Black and Indigenous people, especially those who are poor, trans, or disabled, and we don't all wake up every day and physically do something to change that. Twitter, Instagram, and Facebook give anyone with access to a wi-fi signal a free platform upon which to make public declarations of values and about what we believe matters, and we do. In moments of public conversation about systemic violence, we see heightened levels of political statements, artwork, and infographics—like so many flare signals—as proof of outrage, concern, and solidarity.

But it's also common for those not already committed to ongoing antiracism work, for instance, to go back to business as usual when the news cycle shifts or the media blitz dies down. In much the same way as someone who promises to quit drinking after every alcohol-fueled crisis falls back on the bottle when the crisis subsides, it's common for those with the privilege to do so to forget about resolutions to "do better" in solidarity with victims of injustice. And just as in a clinical setting it is rarely considered *enough* for a person to simply say they want to quit drinking, it is not enough to say something matters to us if we don't consistently act like it. The pentacles suit shows us that values are entwined with the physical domain of our experience, which means that a value isn't just something you feel or believe, it is something you do.

Behavioral therapies are rooted in the study of behavior, which means that they can actually be really good at helping us understand the mechanics of change, how it happens, and how it can get blocked or undermined. Though these therapies tend to focus on individual change, they can be applied to support social change as well. The "evidence-based" part of these therapies is the body of data gathered from observing how people behave, which gives us information about ways to modify behavior. Values are a huge part of many behavioral therapies and therapeutic work in general. In acceptance and commitment therapy (ACT), for instance, clarifying the things we hold precious is considered a foundational part of any work toward modifying behavior.

In ACT, one of the first things you do is identify your values, or what's precious to you. I've always assumed the idea behind this is that you're more likely to do the hard work that change requires if you have a solid sense of *why* you're doing it. Which makes sense. In the counseling field, it's taken for granted that this phase of the process is only the beginning. Imagine if in therapy you could just say what mattered to you and then be done. No, you spend time envisioning what you'd like life to look like and why so that you can notice any discrepancies between that dream and how you've been acting. And then you carefully consider what resources—internal and external—it will take to start to change your behavior and make different choices, ones that are more in line with your best interests and the interests of the community to which you belong.

I think most of us would agree that it would be silly to go to therapy and assume declaring your values was enough to constitute therapeutic success. Progress, maybe, but not enough to say, "We're done here." Defining what's precious is a first step, not to be mistaken for the journey itself. And yet, when it comes to the collective healing process, we make that mistake all the time. We act as though announcing what matters to us is the same thing as living as if it were so. I think we should normalize thinking about values as something that is both ideological and behavioral, as requiring both imagination and will.

A symbol of the feminine, the Queen of Pentacles contains the capacity to dream of this world, and as queen in the earth domain—the realm of behavior—she has the unique ability to marry vision with physical action. The combination of these abilities makes this queen an embodiment of what ACT therapists call values-driven action: behaving as though what you know to be precious is indeed precious. Put another way, worth it to do hard things for. The Queen of Pentacles gazes downward at a pentacle that rests in her lap. Read in the context of capitalist mythology, the coin is a symbol of something that carries worth, and that inward gaze suggests the work of determining what holds true value for her. Not what her mother calls valuable, not what people on social media call valuable, not what she thinks she *should* find valuable, but what really and truly is precious to her.

In *The Book of Thoth*, Aleister Crowley connects the Queen of Pentacles to "the ambition of matter to take part in the Great Work of creation." This is one of the best ways I've come across to describe the experience of being a human who yearns to participate, through values-aligned behavior, in the creation of an ideal world, which may look different depending on whom you talk to. For me, it's a responsive world where cooperation and relationships matter, where resources are channeled to the most vulnerable places, diverse expressions of life and death are honored for the unique roles they play, and activity is determined around a reverence for and defense of what is sacred. The Queen of Pentacles is an invitation to envision what that world is to you and then to choose how you'll participate in creating it.

King of Pentacles

olk interpretations of the pentacles suit typically define it as having to do with career and finance, which in turn symbolize belonging and security. The King of Pentacles often stands for qualities of competence and capability, and though these traits tend to be paired with business achievements and material success, I think they have more to do with the broader human values of feeling safe and knowing where we fit in. The word *capable* comes from both Latin and French words meaning "able to grasp or to hold," which suggests competence is something that requires the wisdom to know the difference between the things within our grasp and the things beyond it. Between what we cannot change, and what we can.

"The wisdom to know the difference" is a line from the Serenity Prayer, which was popularized by Alcoholics Anonymous and other twelve-step recovery programs. These programs also teach the concept of *unmanageability*, which author Melody Beattie writes "occurs when we stop owning our power and start believing that we do not have choices about how we want to act, regardless of what another person is or isn't doing." Unmanageability is, in other words, the antithesis of the King of Pentacles' competence. It refers to what happens when we focus too much on trying to control or manage the dominions of others—behaviors, thoughts, feelings, preferences, opinions—often at the cost of neglecting our own. The fact that the King of Pentacles is situated in a lush garden suggests that it's here—in his own space—that he's most able to access his characteristic traits of competence and capability.

If the King of Pentacles could speak, I think he'd say that competence comes through working in the domains immediately accessible to us. I think he'd say that sometimes when we feel powerless, it's because we're trying to exert influence over domains we don't have rightful access to. Because we're trying to control how other people think and feel and what they do. He'd say that if you're obsessing about how your neighbors' tomatoes won't grow while neglecting your own seedlings, that doesn't make you incapable. You're just trying to manage something you have no control over.

Learning to mind your own business in this particular way takes dedication, which is why it's the wisdom held by a king. It can take a lot of dogged redirecting, especially if you've been habituated to focus more on others' wants and needs than your own. Thankfully, this king offers a down-to-earth, practical instruction: Our power lives in our willingness and ability to attend to our own domains, our own energy, feelings, behaviors, and thoughts. So if you want to feel capable, work on building the capacity to attend to those things without giving in to the impulse to shut down or look away.

Get out your trowel and do some digging. Find coping and distress-tolerance skills that work for you. Experiment just like you would with a vegetable or herb garden. Practice keeping your attention on what you can immediately touch, feel, grasp, hold, and ultimately transform. Melody Beattie's advice is also a good aid here—when you find yourself clinging to something that's making you feel powerless, ask, What do I need to do to take care of myself right now? And then do it. And that's king behavior.

Ace of Swords

ach of the four suits in tarot represents one of four primary domains of our being: energetic, emotional, behavioral, and intellectual. The aces represent the suit in its raw form, a gift given to each of us at birth. The Ace of Swords says, "Welcome to the world, human. And congratulations! You have a mind that can think and reason, evaluate and judge, sort and label, compare and contrast." This ability will help you make decisions for yourself, to know when to say yes and when to say no. But beware, the sword can trap you as quickly as it can cut you out of tight spaces. It is rigid; its two-sided blade tends to see only black and white, and rarely gray. So you'll need to learn some techniques to work well with it.

The spiritual journey of the tarot is about a return to totality, a space beyond pairs of opposites that can accommodate individual and collective, self and other, this and that. The sword's double edge might seem at odds with this idea of totality since it is a symbol of opposing forces, of division, of dualism. But let's remember that at the heart of the spiritual philosophy of tarot is the idea that nothing is all good or all bad. This, paradoxically, is also true for "black-and-white" thinking. Sometimes, seeing things in a straightforward, yes-or-no, this-or-that way can be beneficial. There are times when our evolution depends on the ability to step back from our energetic, emotional, and behavioral experience and simply observe so that we can discern the next step forward. The swords suit can teach us how to do that.

Here's an example from the mythic hero's journey that might help illustrate a time when the sword comes in handy. A hero sets out on a path toward treasure. It doesn't take long before the hero encounters a threshold guardian, some ogre or demon whose sole purpose is to distract, harm, or block the hero's way forward. It would probably be an impediment to the hero's survival and continuance on the path if the hero were to say, "this ogre is not a bad creature, he's been traumatized, he simply knows no other way of life." Though this may be true, it might not be all that helpful in terms of getting the hero beyond the monstrous being and staying focused on the mission. Sometimes, the hero benefits from the type of binary thinking that asks, "Will the choice I'm about to make bring me closer to or further away from what I'm after?" We see that in the stories, and we see it in our lives. There's a ruthlessness to it. The key is knowing when to wield that weapon, and how not to get carried away with it.

As with all the domains of our experience, practice and development are required to cultivate the kind of knife skills needed in order to move wisely, maintain flexibility, and not lose sight of the fact that however useful it may be to sort and categorize, reality is generally ambiguous. Most of the things we encounter in life exist in a gray area. Evelyn Underhill wrote that when the logical mind encounters gray spaces, it "becomes dazed, uncertain of itself; for it is no longer doing its natural work, which is to help life, not to know it."

When we give in to the tendency to categorize things as all good or all bad and draw our swords at inappropriate times, splitting complex, nuanced experiences into rigid evaluative dimensions, the mind goes from being a helpful aid to a liability, like carrying a knife for self-defense that gets turned back on you because you didn't take the proper time to learn to use it. Conversely, when we know how and when to draw the blade—like when we're getting distracted and need sharp focus or have become entangled in a trap of some kind—that's what it's there for, why it stays on our hip, ready. As is the case with all of what tarot teaches us, the ideal is moving flexibly between these modes, as the present moment calls for. The sword isn't going to be the right tool for every challenge in life, but it will be for some.

Two of Swords

ou will probably never hear me say that your thoughts determine your reality because as much as I find things like cognitive reframing and restructuring useful, I think it's misguided to put the entire onus for change on an individual without also holding the environment accountable, acknowledging the ways that things like oppression and violence profoundly impact a person's well-being. And while it's true that changing the way you think about resources can help you access your power, that shift isn't going to magically dissolve very real, systemic barriers that may stand between you and the resources that are available.

And still, our thoughts certainly affect our realities. The stories we carry do—as Mary Van Hook said—shape our lives, and this is why there's a whole suit in tarot dedicated to the domain of thought. Our minds can create incredibly compelling narratives, and there's skill required if we want to use our intellect to our advantage and not as a means to our downfall.

One of the most effective lessons that I've come across for understanding the mind is that we usually cannot block unwanted thoughts. This is important because there's a lot of frustration that comes with wishing anxious, fearful, or obsessive thoughts would go away. Willing a thought to disappear or stop coming is just, unfortunately, not how thoughts work. But I do believe that we have some say in the thoughts we give weight to—the ones we choose to speak aloud or to incorporate into our dominant narratives. And this is where we have to hone our knife skills, where we have to cultivate a bit of cunning. Cunning is described by the poet Robert Bly as—and I'm paraphrasing—the rearranging that is necessary in order to stay in contact with what one knows to be true. Sometimes that's rearranging a material reality, sometimes an internal one, like a narrative.

A narrative I often see that generally doesn't do much good for people is the one in which we repeatedly say—to ourselves and those around us—things like "I have no idea" and "I really don't know" and "I'm just so confused." I shared earlier in this book that confusion is important, that it can be therapeutic (see the Moon on page 107). But confusion is best in brief doses; it's the kind of place you might hike out to for the day to catch a glimpse of something new, but maybe not a place where you should set up camp.

There's too much in this world that we have no control over already for us to be positioning ourselves as powerless over things that we do have a choice in. Sometimes you need to lift your head up, roll your shoulders back, and act like you know. I hear a lot of people say they're confused when what they really mean is "I'm too scared to admit what I know, or to do what that knowing requires of me." And hey, that's okay. I see the person in the Two of Swords as a classic example of this—two swords over the chest protect the heart, the first thing in the line of fire when a tough choice is made.

Indecision can be protective, just as keeping that blindfold on can be protective. Holding those two heavy swords still like that can't be easy, but perhaps it feels safer than making an actual choice and just going for it. It's not always only that we don't want to face the reality of what we know. Sometimes, we find comfort in confusion and indecision because we believe that if we were to accept reality, we would not be capable of managing the emotions that would come up. Here's where the sword needs to come out, where you need to get to some rearranging. To keep contact with what you know to be true.

Arthur Waite's and Aleister Crowley's interpretations of this card say it's to do with friendship and peace, respectively, and I don't think that's too far off from the reflections here. We form an alliance with ourselves by choosing narratives that are supportive and empowering rather than disparaging. If you wouldn't describe a friend who was hesitating to act on what they knew to be true as "confused" or "lost," maybe don't talk about yourself that way either.

Three of Swords

Difficult emotions tend not to come alone. Psychologist Edward Teyber says that hard feelings sometimes come in clusters of three, and the one we're most comfortable with takes the lead, shielding us from those we have a tougher time processing. The leading emotion is different for everyone. For some, anger takes the lead and creates a shield from deep sadness. It isn't that sadness is inherently tougher to feel or process than anger, but perhaps that it is coupled with a third feeling, shame, around having been rejected in sad moments as a child. Other people may be more able to express sadness because they see their anger as too dreadful. Expressing or even feeling fury might be accompanied by overwhelming guilt.

Teyber says that change becomes possible when we're able to come to grips with each feeling in the triad—the sadness, the anger, and the guilt or shame—making way for each to be safely expressed. And it doesn't necessarily need to be resolved right then and there, but the idea is to bring those feelings from the underground to the surface. Where we can have a better shot at working with them.

One sword would be sufficient to illustrate heartbreak, but in this card we see three. A central sword might represent the emotion we tend to lead with, but it's not the whole story, just as expressions of anger or sadness rarely give us a full picture of what lies beneath. The two swords on each side symbolize emotions that might sit under or alongside screaming in rage or crying in despair, ones that are often harder to express because they are either less tolerable, were seen as less acceptable in childhood, or both. That the Three of Swords includes all three tells us that all three are important, and all three may need to be addressed so that the heart can heal. Address rage and you will often find deep grief, guilt, or shame waiting to be acknowledged as well.

When dealing with difficult emotions, you want to find a way to feel each feeling in the cluster. There are many ways to call up emotions, through journaling, dance, dialogue, art, or spiritual practice. If you're planning to do this, keep in mind that you've been defending against the scariest emotions for a reason, so learning to feel them will require discernment, patience, and compassion for yourself. We learned in the cups suit that emotions are like water in that they can flood and overwhelm us, draw our feet from the ground, and sweep us away. Imagine that you are on the beach dipping into the ocean. Pay close attention to the currents, don't go farther out than you'll be safe to go, and if necessary, ally yourself with a professional—a lifeguard type—who can ensure you stay afloat when the waves get strong.

Feeling hard feelings in the presence of someone you trust can keep you grounded in the moment and will provide the reparative experience of feeling all of your emotions without the risk of rejection or abandonment. One of the ways we can take the charge out of the feelings we're most afraid of is by staying with them. So when a hard feeling comes up, look it square in the eye and let it know you're scared but not chicken. Watch for dysfunctional coping mechanisms here, like wanting to fall back on an emotion-saturated narrative like one of anger or despair, victimization or hopelessness. Watch for urges to use a numbing behavior or escape strategy; it's really common to see those here. Self-soothing when things get too painful is not the same as avoiding. Keep something tactile on hand to help you ground in the physical—a cozy blanket, a frozen orange to hold, lotion with a calming scent—that'll keep you anchored on shore when the waves start to swell.

Remember that learning to tolerate distress is a marathon, not a sprint. No one's grading or timing you, so go at your own pace and reserve the right to take breaks. As you start to build up tolerance with the really tough stuff, you can challenge yourself to feel the hardest feelings for two minutes without using a numbing or avoidance strategy, then two hours, four hours, six. As you go, I think you'll learn some important secrets about the life span of the really intense ones.

Positive psychology research has suggested that it's not the amount of happiness, but the range of emotions we have the capacity to feel that predicts well-being. People who only know how to express anger often find themselves increasingly isolated because anger is often unpleasant, scary, or difficult for others to be around. Sadness tends to invite compassion, but when it dominates our experience, it creates a sense of helplessness that, too, makes life small. Shame and guilt can function inside the human mind and body like a poison, concealing parts of our experience that need sunlight to live, depositing invisible land mines that we wind up doing elaborate rituals to avoid. The emotions are distinct, but the medicine for each is essentially the same: as we learned in the cups suit, emotions have a life cycle of their own that begs to be honored. Our minds are so powerful, known to wield swords to defend against feelings that are too tough to bear, and so our work is to notice the ways in which we haven't made space and create that so that emotions do not become lodged in the heart, in turn keeping us stuck in old thoughts, feelings, and behaviors that betray our growth and well-being.

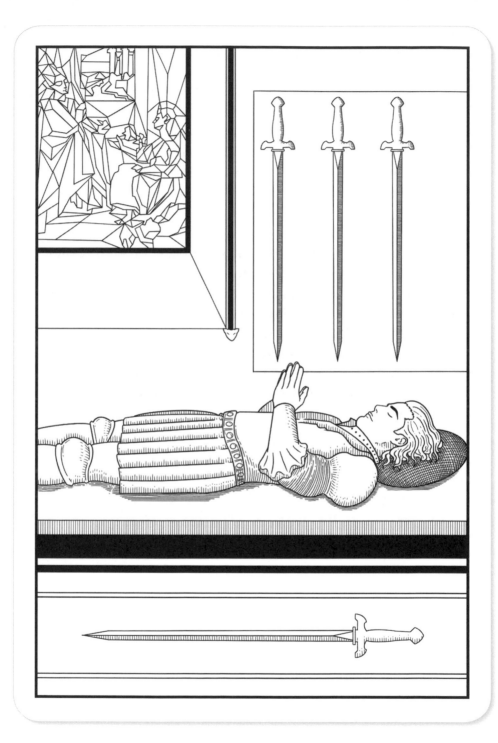

Four of Swords

n the swords suit more than any other, we're reminded that words—a product of the thinking mind—can be both a medicine and a poison. The narratives we carry can diminish or empower us, bring us from decrepitude to strength and vice versa. One of my favorite stanzas, which I consider to be a powerful medicine for the experience of loneliness, was written by the Persian poet Ḥāfez:

Don't surrender your loneliness so quickly.
Let it cut more deep.
Let it ferment and season you
as few human and even divine ingredients can.

These words take an experience that so many people suffer and struggle with, and inject it with the power to heal. They are a reminder that loneliness, like all difficult emotions, is itself a kind of portal for us to pass through and come out changed. It is an opening to do magic, to go in deep and emerge later transformed—fermented, seasoned—perhaps returning with a benediction of some kind.

Some of the old interpretations of the Four of Swords say that it's a card about atonement. I read once that before battle, a knight with the means to do so would have a sarcophagus made, should he perish while fighting. If he survived, he would come home, lie in the tomb, and ask forgiveness. This was his way of making amends or atoning after war, for any lives he'd taken or crimes he'd committed.

For us, too, after we've gone off somewhere—maybe into a new relationship or some other journey that, at least at first, felt promising—it's often not until we're back home, alone with ourselves, that we can see with painful clarity the ways in which we have outsourced our own safety and care, or pawned off the tenderest parts of ourselves onto others. Earnest hopes that a new person or situation will finally give us the security or care we've always yearned for can be like a cloud that fogs our judgment, causing us to surrender responsibility for ourselves when we are meant to retain it. That particular type of haze can lead us to give too much of ourselves over to others in a way that is compulsive, reckless, against our better judgment. And in doing so, we might incur wounds not only to ourselves but to all involved. As a result, by the time we make it back home, we may feel disoriented, out of control, or ashamed.

Once we are alone, we may look at our lack of competence in caring for ourselves and find it terrifying, and that's when that urge to run often makes its grand and grizzly appearance. Faced with its bearlike presence, we have a choice: we can either continue acting out the futile cycle of seeking to outsource the care we so desperately need or get going with the task of working with our fears and loneliness differently. Maybe leaning in further this time, listening to them long enough that we might use them to learn. I've noticed, and perhaps you have, too, there's a certain glow about people who've chosen the latter and really committed to it. They have a look to them like the soft orange windows of a lonely hunter's cabin after dark, nestled into a remote notch between mountains.

Poet David Whyte wrote that "in the wild, the best response to dangerous circumstances is often not to run but to assume a profoundly attentive identity, to pay attention to what seems to threaten and, in that attention, not to assume the identity of the victim." Which comes back to what I love so much about Ḥāfez's take on loneliness, and why I view his poem as medicine. Though it can feel threatening, even terrifying, we have a choice to relate to loneliness as an ingredient that might do wonderful things to us, that can "ferment and season" us like nothing else, if we can let it.

Whyte continues, "Through being equal to fierce circumstances we make ourselves larger than the part of us that wants to flee while not losing its protective understandings about when it might be appropriate." Because sometimes we do need to run, but the swords—their double edge symbolizing choice and discernment—remind us that we always have the power to make decisions, to decide when running or when staying will yield the most life.

Five of Swords

Though I generally think about the cups as relating to our capacity for dreaming and imagination, the swords suit also has to do with imagination in that it symbolizes our ability to generate meaning through narrative and storytelling that may not exist otherwise. As we move through the swords suit, we hear secrets about both the potentials and pitfalls of having a mind that processes reality through the stringing together of words about it, and the ways in which we can use this ability to our advantage or detriment. For me, the images found within the swords suit are teeming with concepts from cognitive and narrative therapies, since these therapies approach healing through the domain of thoughts and with deep reverence for the power of stories. As mythologist Martin Shaw has written, "Bad storytellers make spells. Great storytellers break them."

In his *Pictorial Key to the Tarot*, Arthur Waite wrote that the Five of Swords signified themes of revocation, dishonor, and loss. Each of these words falls under the umbrella of failure, but because the card is a part of the swords suit, and so chock-full of ambiguity, there is a lot of space for interpretation. Depending on which of the three characters in the card you identify with, the card could be victory, but it could also be defeat. I've read interpretations that say both. Simply engaging with this card is an experiential lesson in the unique capacity of the intellect to make meaning out of not-yet-named things. There's always an option to tell a more or less empowering version of a story.

When we go to a healer of any kind, we always bring a tale. Usually that story has been pared down to a version that is succinct and oversimplified. The key points, the crux of the thing, the core com-plaints. The truncation and thinning of stories is endemic in our cul-ture because of the way our healthcare system is set up to maximize efficiency and productivity. You paid for fifty minutes of healing, so you'd better get to the point and make it snappy. But I think true heal-ing depends on an understanding of the dynamic and contextual na-ture of our stories. When we make problems into elevator speeches, we're choosing a psychic location for ourselves—"I am broken, I am damaged, I have been victimized"—and setting up shop there. If that stance is not one of agency or power, we start to see our lives through that perspective, and the brain's confirmation bias excludes anything to the contrary. "I am broken and am blind to any evidence that I am whole. I am damaged and therefore cannot see physical proof that I am perfect in my complexities. I am a victim, I cannot see my power."

Cognitive behavioral therapy (CBT) is based on the notion that thoughts—whether true or untrue—can and often do stimulate feel-ings that can in turn trigger certain behaviors in order to cope with those feelings. Sometimes when you trace a compulsive behavior back to where it came from, you find there was a hidden belief about being unworthy or unlovable at its root. Narrative therapy also approaches healing through the avenue of intellect, by uplifting the importance of stories in shaping life and supporting the building out and *thickening* of narrow or incomplete narratives. Both CBT and narrative therapy draw on the power we have to intentionally generate thoughts that highlight and make space for personal power, sovereignty, and strength in addition to any existing narratives about obstacles, vulnerabilities, or personal shortcomings.

All stories, for the most part, are incomplete; anytime you are a storyteller, you are also a magician in that you are drawing attention to one thing in part by diverting it from another. Stories by nature don't contain the whole narrative; they can't. In order to smooth out the texture of a story—to make it easier for telling to ourselves or others—we conveniently omit perspectives that might complicate things. One of the jobs of the storytelling mind is to make life compre-hensible, which means sorting, labeling, and categorizing. But don't forget that the Fool's journey is one of occupying the edges, where nothing is all this or that, all good or bad.

So much of what we see is a matter of how we frame and define it through the filter of the intellectual mind. We always have at least some amount of choice in whether we say, "I tried and failed," or, "I tried and learned." There's a deep ambiguity to failure that we are wise to be aware of. Every failure, every experience of revocation, dishonor, or loss, holds inside of it an opportunity for growth. And while you are never—and I repeat, *never*—required to frame a traumatic experience as an opportunity, you always, always, always have the option to tell a story that highlights your agency and power.

Six of Swords

reaking patterns is hard. If it weren't, they wouldn't be patterns in the first place. When we look under the hood of the patterns that don't serve us, we often find a current of emotions that we've been trying to keep at bay. Left unexamined, the impulse to avoid certain internal experiences can fuel the continued choosing of a thing that breeds suffering. This is why simply knowing that a pattern is happening is often insufficient for actual change. Usually, we have to summon the willingness to feel something that we simply weren't willing to feel before.

Awareness of a pattern is a great starting point, for sure. Once you've identified that a pattern is happening, you can start to see where the fear is living; it's often at the exact location where the pattern could be broken. Each time you hit the edge of a feeling that scares you, you're at a crossroads with a choice to make. Either you can keep walking that well-worn path that allows you to avoid the thing you're scared of, or you can choose a new route. If you haven't cultivated the willingness and skill to engage with feelings that scare you, you're likely to take the same old route you're used to.

Importantly, we rarely *feel* like breaking a pattern or doing a new behavior. You're not going to be in the mood to feel the fear, anxiety, guilt, or terror that tends to accompany new growth. These things are inherently hard to hold. As artist Carolyn Lazard has written, "The thing about pain is that it's pain." But Lazard goes on to say that "[pain] is a generative sensation because it always, without a doubt, motivates you to get away from it, to end it by any means necessary." *Generative* is defined as "relating to or capable of production or reproduction." And, for sure, pain can drive us to produce behaviors whose sole purpose is to move us *away* from it. But it can also nudge us *toward* something precious, if we're willing to be with it a bit. And this is where a little practice called "doing the opposite" comes in.

I started studying tarot while working in self-help book publishing, and I remember pulling the Six of Swords and thinking of an exercise from acceptance and commitment therapy (ACT) in which a person imagines they're driving a bus full of loud and disparaging monsters on the road toward something that matters to the driver. The monsters are meant to represent the unruly and at times overwhelming internal chorus of characters like self-doubt, self-criticism, and inadequacy. The bus symbolizes our personal vehicle, the physical body; the road is the life journey; and the driver is the "higher" observing self, who has the choice either to take orders from the obnoxious and demanding passengers or to stick to the route as planned. The metaphor is meant to help people recognize that while it may not be possible to get rid of difficult internal experiences like anxiety—to kick them "off the bus," so to speak—it is fully possible to get better at bringing them along for the ride toward what matters without letting them boss us around. Just as a hero must move through obstacles on the way toward some treasure—like Odysseus making his way back to Ithaca, past Cyclopes, temptresses, and lotus-eaters—we, too, must move through internal obstacles on our way toward what's personally meaningful.

In the Six of Swords, a woman and child set out toward a better life. A character stands behind them, steering, like the driver in the ACT metaphor—perhaps a "higher" wise self who knows where to go and what must be endured in order to get there. The boat is moving forward, but it is studded with swords, symbolizing prickly psychological experiences that, while sharp, heavy, and often difficult to hold, are a necessary part of the process. Pluck them out and the boat—now riddled with holes—will sink. This detail adds an important layer of insight into the vital nature of fear, and the role it plays in living a meaningful life. It suggests that fear is not just a thing to be tolerated but in fact an indelible part of living in alignment with what's precious. In exploring the pros and cons of living a meaningful life, researchers have found data to suggest that those who identified as having meaningful work and relationships were also more likely to experience fear of failure and worry about loss than their counterparts who did not.

So if you're afraid about making some change, maybe you've touched on something precious. Dennis Tirch, a psychologist and friend who specializes in compassion-focused approaches to healing, once said that if you wait for every part of you to be on board with some big change, you'll be waiting a long time. Indeed, that temptation to wait for fear to subside is a trap. The fear is the cost of admission.

Seven of Swords

rauma therapist Laurie Kahn wrote that "one of the cruelest truths about childhood trauma is the way it revisits its victims when they are adults." Unresolved trauma seeks resolution through the re-creation of painful dynamics from the past, and it is often after this process has repeated too many times to be coincidence that a person finally seeks help. Often that help is something a person has to continually seek as layers peel back and back, restoring the capacity to choose people, places, and things that do not promise repeated pain and suffering.

In her book about victims of childhood abuse, which is aptly titled *Baffled by Love*, Kahn writes of "Little Red Riding Hood," the popular tale of a young girl so out of touch with her instinctual sense of what is safe and unsafe that she mistakes a ravenous wolf dressed in an old woman's clothing for her grandmother. In early versions of the story, the girl is eaten alive. In later ones, she's rescued by a lumberjack. Kahn uses this story to illustrate the concept of *betrayal blindness*, which can plague adult survivors of childhood abuse; it starts out adaptive, a protective mechanism that helps a kid maintain a relationship with a caregiver who both hurts them and upon whom they depend for survival. But in adulthood it becomes maladaptive, it gives the victim blinders when they need to be seeing clearly, often making way for the repetition of abuse.

I think the lumberjack in the story represents a more functional and adaptive defense that develops with time and healing. The part that sees that gray mangy tail sticking out the back of someone's clothes, and the long curly claws where toenails should be, and says, "Oh, no thank you, not today, I'd better be going." The part that not only sees but also processes a red flag properly, a guidepost on a very specific path toward a very particular kind of suffering, and that makes the call then and there to turn back.

The Seven of Swords is often read as a card of deceit or betrayal. A person with a tricksterish gait has five swords in hand as he steals away, looking over his shoulder lest he be caught and found out to be a thief. Sure, we often can't help but view this card as an omen or warning sign that trickery is afoot somewhere among those we're close to. But we can also see it as an invitation to identify the part of our own psychology that says, "Hey, look over there!" when we should be looking right here. The part that pulls the wool down over our own eyes and that distorts information as a matter of some old, outdated relational habit. This line of inquiry offers a pathway toward understanding what in us drives the urge to forge relationships with those who can't be trusted in the first place and gives us something to work with in ourselves.

Eight of Swords

ne of the key concepts in cognitive behavioral therapy (CBT) is that we all have core beliefs, unconscious ideas that form the bedrock of our understanding about who we are, who others are, and how the world is. A major task in CBT is identifying core beliefs, looking at how they influence our thoughts and how those thoughts then influence our emotions, which, in turn, influence behavior. Core beliefs can be similar to what author Michael A. Singer calls "thorns," razor-like internal formations that can cause excruciating pain when rubbed up against or touched. As a result, we unconsciously build our whole lives and behavioral lexicons around avoiding anything that might brush up against these thorny core beliefs. A person who carries a core belief that they're unlovable, for example, might create a rule to avoid intimacy in order to avoid having to feel the prick of unlovability in a close relationship. That rule might manifest as an unconscious gravitation toward unavailable partners, abstaining from dating altogether, or even social isolation. Before we're aware of these thorns, many of us will do anything to avoid being pricked by them. Even when it makes life small.

Rigid adherence to these rules is called *experiential avoidance*, which is exactly what it sounds like—avoiding certain experiences, sometimes internal and sometimes external, all in an effort to protect ourselves from thinking, feeling, or experiencing anything that we believe we cannot handle. I've rarely if ever seen a better illustration of this concept than in the Eight of Swords. It captures everything from the sharpness of the thorns to that hemmed-in feeling you get when you believe there are certain things that are not safe to think, feel, or experience. Having been here many times myself, I can speak to the precision with which this image depicts what it's like when, in all cardinal directions, there are feelings you're not willing to feel and thorns you believe might bleed you dry at the slightest touch. If this person were to remove the blindfold—to be willing to see and deal with whatever is there in the present moment—they would realize that there are many ways to engage with a sharp thing other than to build a life around avoiding it.

You might start out by making an honest appraisal of which swords—or psychological experiences—you're most scared of and how that affects and ultimately constricts your range of motion. Oftentimes, you might feel that you're stuck between a rock and hard place—there are two sets of unpleasant feelings, one on either side, that you're having to choose between. When you're feeling trapped like this, it can seem as if there's no way to win, since no matter which direction you go, there is pain. Life is like that sometimes.

But here's a thing to consider: generally, there will be one set of feelings in a situation like this that you're more comfortable with. For example, for the person who fears intimacy, loneliness isn't pleasant, but it feels safe to a degree because it's familiar. If that person chooses the route of loneliness, their growth is limited because they're not going anywhere they haven't been. The set of feelings in the other direction might involve contact with old wounds around closeness and self-worth, and seeing how those wounds come up in close relationships. This second route may be a lot more terrifying, understandably. But at least there is space to grow there, room for new learning. And it's always good to remember that in these situations, *you have a choice*. You get to decide what getting unstuck is worth to you. You get to choose what, when, and how you're willing to feel what needs to be felt in order for movement to happen.

Nine of Swords

The goal of acceptance and commitment therapy (ACT) is psychological flexibility, which is defined by psychologist Steven Hayes as "the ability to contact the present moment more fully as a conscious human being, and to change or persist in behavior when doing so serves valued ends." I think about it as the ability to move continuously in the direction of one's values even in the face of internal obstacles. In the ACT model, there is a set of six processes that are believed to support this kind of flexibility, one of which is called *defusion*, which Hayes says results in "a decrease in believability of, or attachment to, private events rather than an immediate change in their frequency."

The idea with defusion is that while you may not be able to stop the occurrence of difficult internal events, you can learn to step back from them so as to diminish the power they have over your behavior. Conversely, when we're fused with anxious thoughts, we take the thoughts as facts, and therefore do whatever it is they might be telling us to do: skip the social gathering, take the longer route to work so we don't have to go over the bridge, avoid the tough conversation. In the Nine of Swords, we see a person sitting up in bed with their face in their hands and swords driving through the crown, throat, and chest. This person is so fused with the swords—with their thoughts or other internal events—that they can't see anything else. If this person could just pull back a bit, get some space instead of closing in on and around the swords, they might find some room to move in a way that would feel right. They might find some flexibility.

Because thoughts and feelings are so incredibly compelling, we have a natural tendency to take them super seriously and either cling to the ones we do want or turn away from the ones we don't in a sort of knee-jerk way. Defusion can help in both of these cases by inserting points of choice where it previously seemed there were none. If you can see a thought or feeling happen, that means you've created space between yourself and whatever your mind is doing. That's defusion, and it's going to protect you on the path toward the life you want by providing you a bit of space from any internal ogres or seducers you may encounter on the road.

Defusion is not easy to do, and it definitely takes practice, but because it's such a lucky charm with so many protective benefits, a lot's been done to determine the best ways to learn it. It's totally possible to get good enough at defusing that when you're sitting up in bed, getting poked and prodded ruthlessly by the sharp blades of anxious or despairing thoughts, you can make some spaciousness. Here are some of my favorite techniques: Ask yourself whether it's possible to have the thought you're having and behave in a contrary way. Ask yourself who these thoughts serve, in whose or what house do they worship. Narrate the story of your mind in the present, say, "My mind is saying I'm going to fail this test tomorrow, my mind is saying no one will ever love me." Thank your mind for staying on the job, reliably, 24-7 without any sick days. After all, even if it *is* incredibly loud and obnoxious, it's only doing what it thinks you need in order to protect you. Let your mind know that it can take a break, and that as a token of your deep appreciation, you'll take it from here.

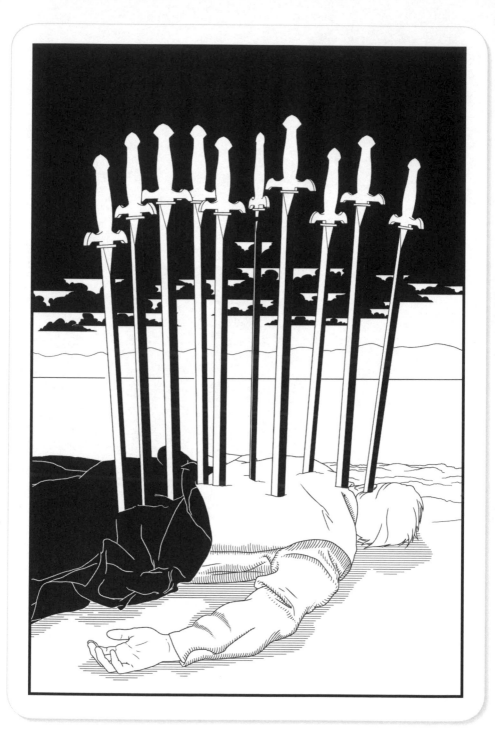

Ten of Swords

he fourth step in the twelve-step model for recovery includes making a "moral and fearless inventory," a stocktaking practice in which you're invited to list all resentments, fears, grudges, and weapons formed against you, real or perceived. Essentially, you give yourself full permission and encouragement to create an exhaustive list of everything anyone's ever done to you that's caused you harm or injury. How often in your life have you been given that kind of permission? Do you notice any immediate thoughts or judgments coming up as you consider it?

Life is full of painful experiences, so if the thought of recalling and listing every single one feels overwhelming at first, it might help to choose a focus. Maybe, if the idea of creating such an inventory feels valuable, you could choose to focus on resentments and wounds from a particular time in life. The aim is ambitious: to clear the backlog of all that's built up and to release ourselves once and for all from the weight of what's kept us pinned to the earth and to the past, stuck at the scene of some aging, old crime.

Letting go doesn't happen on demand. That's because willpower is not a medicine and it does not heal wounds. If you broke your leg as a child and never received proper medical care, it would be no surprise if you have trouble walking as an adult. And yet with psychological wounds, the go-to method is so often to will them away and then proceed to find increasingly creative and elaborate ways of avoiding, blaming, and beating ourselves up for the ways in which our painful early experiences have hindered our ability to live well. This practice of taking inventory is one of many possible first steps toward treating wounds that never received proper care.

The swords in tarot symbolize the ability to narrate and intellectualize, and thus teach us about the ways in which we can use this capacity to evolve. If you have ever grown hot with rage or heavy with despair simply by thinking about something painful—whether past, present, or future—then you already know the immense power of the thinking, verbal mind. Thoughts are so powerful that they can stimulate intense emotional states that permeate our entire experience. The Ten of Swords—with its image of a person laid out beneath the crushing weight of many swords—is a good illustration of what this can look like whether the thoughts are true, half-true, or flat-out wrong. I suspect that this is why the practice of taking inventory can be so powerful for some. It's cathartic, a way to summon the hot stuff that can rage uncontained if we don't make a proper space for it, give it a ring or a hearth to blaze safely inside. Keep in mind that the sword is the symbol of discernment; judgment is always needed when deliberately summoning fire. Do not go alone beyond what you're equipped to cope with on your own. Tell someone you trust where you're going. Line up supports, to be safe.

Often where we get into trouble is when a thought stimulates an intense feeling, and then, in order to avoid that feeling, we turn to a maladaptive coping strategy. This behavior—a reaction to an emotion triggered by a thought—generates more pain for us. Meanwhile, we never paused to ask whether the original thought was true or useful. Sometimes when you feel really bad, you can trace the feelings back to a thought or set of thoughts. "I'm a failure, no one likes me, I'll be alone forever." Absolute statements—and the Ten of Swords just screams absolutes—are always suspect, and therefore a great place to start.

The practice of taking inventory, on the other hand, is one way to use the power of thought to stimulate latent emotions, on purpose and for healing. By calling up memories—with discernment, always, and full permission to back off the moment it gets to feel like too much—we summon up unresolved feelings that are associated with them in a way that can be safe and empowered. We let ourselves feel the weight of

330

them on and in the body. In a culture obsessed with moving on, it's wild how rare an opportunity it is to really dwell down deep at the bottom of a loss. This card is often read as one of an absolute ending, and I think that's a nod to the potential in this practice for real letting go to be possible. And it is far from the only way. Just one way of many to consider.

Page of Swords

he essence of the swords suit is that we each have the ability to think, evaluate, and reason, but that these abilities can either liberate or imprison us, depending on the time and effort we take to learn to use them skillfully. The swords court—the page, knight, queen, and king—provides a beautiful and clear visual depiction of this process of learning how to use the swords skillfully: from the reactive page to the focused knight, discerning queen, and still, stoic king.

In the Bhagavad Gita, one of the world's most influential spiritual texts, Lord Krishna gives this wisdom to the hero-warrior Arjuna about the importance of training the mind:

> The senses wander, and when one lets the mind follow them, it
> carries wisdom away like a windblown ship on the waters.

Today, our evidence-based therapy models incorporate mindfulness, many going so far as to be called "mindfulness based," meaning that they are rooted in the ancient technology of learning to both focus the mind in the present and witness the activity of the mind rather than experience its activity as the self. In acceptance and commitment therapy (ACT), for example, the self is *context*, not content.

Mindfulness exercises performed in clinical settings are done with the hope that rather than react immediately to every thought and feeling that passes through, a person who learns to observe the mind is able to widen the gap between stimulus and response; they can see a thought before reacting to it, experience a bit of distance from it, and thereby become less reactive. From there, they are able to move with greater intention and connection to their values.

Tarotist Lon Milo DuQuette has written that when we identify with the swords domain of our experience—the cognitive intellectual—we "rise above and separate ourselves from our lower nature, the animal soul." But that when we overidentify with the intellect, in other words, when we are too attached to the mind and its thoughts, "we also separate ourselves from the higher parts of our souls that represent greater realities and levels of consciousness." We alienate ourselves from the stuff of life that transcends intellectual comprehension. French philosopher Henri Bergson has written that "intellect is characterized by a natural inability to comprehend life." So perhaps this is why, when a mystic—or anyone who desires a more authentic experience of reality—realizes they must wage a kind of symbolic "battle" with the mind for the seat of authority, they send in their best warriors. Enter the Page of Swords.

Clouds are a prominent symbol in the illustrations of the swords court, and particularly in the Page of Swords. The metaphor of mental events—thoughts, story lines, judgments—as clouds passing through the sky is a common one. The quote by Buddhist teacher Pema Chödrön comes to mind: "You are the sky. Everything else—it's just the weather." Here we see the Page of Swords with clouds swirling around her—they symbolize future thoughts, past thoughts, anxious thoughts, fearful thoughts, soothing and pleasant thoughts, too. Her sword is drawn in reactivity; she's ready to attack. As the court cards evolve, we'll track this progression and see the way that, with time and practice, a new kind of relationship with the clouds—the contents of the mind—begins to unfold. One that is less adversarial, and more spacious.

With experience, the page will come to realize that the activity of the mind isn't necessarily something to challenge directly (though she will learn that sometimes direct challenge is helpful, and will develop the discernment to know when), but rather that it is something to come into a more flexible relationship with. She will learn that clouds do form and sometimes pour rain, but that getting rid of them isn't a requirement to move forward. She'll see how, if she can hunker down and ride them out, eventually, they dissipate altogether. Over time, as we'll see later with the king, the young warrior who was once ready to do battle at the drop of a hat can quell the need to react at all.

Knight of Swords

housands of years ago, well before Western behavioral science researchers had the idea to measure the benefits of mindfulness meditation, spiritual people in India, China, and Japan were meditating. Ancient masters understood that the practices of focus and concentration were critical to evolution far before Westerners like founder of Mindfulness-Based Stress Reduction Jon Kabat-Zinn began using mindfulness techniques to aid people with chronic illness in the late 1970s. Kabat-Zinn has defined mindfulness as "paying attention in a particular way: on purpose, in the present moment and non-judgmentally."

Mindfulness skills are taught in many contemporary psychotherapies, sometimes as part of a process designed to enhance *psychological flexibility*, or the ability to move in the direction of our values even as difficult thoughts and feelings arise, like monsters popping up to block a hero en route to treasure. To start practicing mindfulness, a therapy client may be instructed to focus on the breath, or on one part of the body. Each time their attention wanders—which it will, tirelessly—they'll be directed to continuously return their attention to the breath or that one part of the body.

Perhaps more than ever, in an age where our attention is literally harvested through social media platforms that make money through advertising, the ability to choose a focus and fix one's gaze there is an imperative psychological skill. As we saw with the Page of Swords, clouds symbolize the activities of the mind, and this symbolism extends throughout the entire swords court. Here, we see the Knight of

Swords surrounded by jagged clouds, their distinct shape suggesting the kind of distraction that's intense and difficult to ignore. Nevertheless, the Knight of Swords charges forward, gaze fixed on what matters. He demonstrates the kind of laser-like focus that mindfulness practice helps us develop, while at the same time revealing just how hard it can be. The path toward what's precious is paved with endless bids for our attention. Through practices that build our capacity to focus, we build the mental muscle that's needed to resist getting pulled too far out where we don't belong.

The Yoga Sutras—believed to have been compiled before 400 CE and which were authored by the mysterious sage (or many sages) who went by the name of Patanjali—teach that mindfulness practice, or "the practice of concentration on a single subject," is "the best way to prevent the obstacles and their accompaniments." In his interpretation of the Yoga Sutras, Sri Swami Satchidananda writes that "the point here is that we should not keep changing our object of concentration. When you decide on one thing, stick to it whatever happens."

Hundreds of years later this wisdom has replicated in behavioral therapies that encourage clients to identify personal values and then choose behaviors that move them toward and not away from those values. Satchidananda continues, "There is no value in digging shallow wells in a hundred places. Decide on one place and dig deep." And whether you're working with the Yoga Sutras, a mindfulness-based behavioral therapy, the tarot, or a combination of the three, the instruction is the same: Identify your values and, as my grandfather would say, "stay the course," whatever happens. Even when the clouds are jagged and the thunder loud, when there is anxiety, loneliness, lust, grief, guilt. Commit, and accept what you need to in order to stay on your path. Fix your gaze and keep going.

Queen of Swords

n a much-loved Russian fairy tale, a young girl named Vasilisa is sent by her wicked stepmother and stepsisters to the deep forest home of the child-eating witch Baba Yaga, to fetch fire. Vasilisa's stepmother and stepsisters are hoping she'll die fulfilling this task, but the young girl brings a magic doll that her birth mother had given her before she passed away, and the doll aids her.

Baba Yaga gives Vasilisa a number of chores, some seemingly impossible—*wash my clothes, clean my house and yard, and separate these molding corn kernels from the good ones*—and as Vasilisa sleeps, the doll does it all. Impressed, the witch then orders Vasilisa to parse poppy seeds from a mound of dirt and divide them into two piles. And once again, as Vasilisa dozes, the doll does the job. With that, Baba Yaga grants Vasilisa fire and sends her home to her stepfamily. The story ends abruptly, as is also often the case in old tales, when the fire burns the wicked stepmother and stepsisters to ash. Vasilisa, of course, is spared.

The task of sifting poppy seeds from dirt is obviously one having to do with discernment, with "separating this from that" as Jungian analyst Clarissa Pinkola Estés says in her telling of the tale in the iconic *Women Who Run with the Wolves*. It is about a high degree of know-how with a sword—knife skills, in other words—because the intellect's double edge is what helps parse out what's good or bad, this or that, black or white. As we've seen throughout the swords suit, this capacity can cause problems for us. But the queen is exalted; she embodies the ability to use her blade for the highest good.

In the story, the fact that all the difficult tasks are completed while Vasilisa is asleep gives a sense that the conscious mind is being over-ridden in favor of a deeper, darker knowing, something that emerges from the rich soil of the unconscious when proper space is made to receive it. No amount of intellectual problem-solving was going to keep Vasilisa alive if she couldn't separate the seeds from the dirt pile, but some other, intuitive part of her knew exactly what to do.

There's a suggestion here that although the sword is naturally lit-eral, does great with explicit tasks, there is more to using it properly than what exists at the surface. To know the physical difference be-tween a seed and a piece of dirt would not have been sufficient; some-thing deeper was needed to complete the task of parsing out what's life giving. Many times in life are like this; facts alone are not sufficient to make a choice.

So what *is* that deeper knowing that's required? I think the clouds near the queen's feet and her receptive posture—hand outstretched as if in welcome—contain some clues. Some call the Queen of Swords cold or unfeeling, but I think more see the image, feel it, and know otherwise. The clouds disclose the secret of a deep and at times tumul-tuous inner life. They suggest that the cool exterior and capacity to wield the blade wisely and precisely at the right moments was hard-won. I personally think this queen passed many times through witches' quarters and forests full of dangerous tasks and trials. Having been through that—the terror, the hopelessness, the heartbreak, the grief... and the relief, too—she came out on the other side with a treasure. Like Vasilisa traipsing through the woods to return home with fire. The magic doll was given to Vasilisa by her mother; I think that means that the doll's powers—and the queen's—derive from experience, age, and the heartbreaks and healing inherent in the passage of time.

I've sometimes thought about the sword as a symbol of discern-ment between temporal reality and a transcendent reality that goes beyond the field of space and time. But there is something very straight-forward about it, too, a suggestion that as time goes on we do become wiser through the things we experience. There is something good about remembering this. With her connection to wisdom and skill, the

Queen of Swords carries the energy of an elder. She is a reminder that we gather secrets as we go. And that through the things we experience, we develop the capacity to separate felt data into knowledge that will aid us in making wise choices for ourselves. We learn to sift the poppy seeds from the dirt, and to use them for nourishment when it feels right to.

King of Swords

n his *Pictorial Key to the Tarot*, Arthur Waite writes that the King of Swords is "the power of life and death." If we consider that each card tells a psychological and spiritual secret in the domain to which it belongs—the swords about the intellectual experience, the cups about the emotional experience, the major arcana about the greater life journey, and so on—the King of the Swords' instruction is that a person should work to develop concentration and the ability to direct and fix attention at will. If this king carries "the power of life and death," his message is that developing a level of mastery with our attention endows us with the power to give life to any situation, and also the power to take it away.

I think a lot about the word *worship* when I think about attention, since to worship something means to give value or worth to it. Because our attention is such a precious resource, and increasingly hard to come by with the constant stimulation of smartphones and social media, we are automatically ascribing worth to something when we put our focus there. To a very real extent, we are worshipping—or giving worth to—anything we put our mind to. When you think of it this way, how does that sit?

The way to harnessing the power of life and death, says the King of Swords, is through developing concentration, and this is done through a practice where you consistently put your focus on something of your choosing and don't move it. A good thing to know going into it is that you're going to move your focus. A lot. I know people who have been meditating for hours a day for decades, and not one of them has mastered the ability to not move it. The point is that you make a commitment to putting your focus somewhere and then to bringing it back as often as you need to. I think the bringing it back is an integral part, where the muscle that lets you continuously come back to what you value bulks up. And this isn't the kind of thing you do once, or for a week, or even for a year and you're good. It needs to be ongoing, a sort of psychological hygiene practice like brushing your teeth.

And aside from bestowing you with the power of life and death, it isn't hard to see how the ability to fix your gaze on an object of your choosing would benefit you on the daily. If you love or believe in something, for example, and want to see it grow, this skill will help you be with that thing more fully, and in a sustained way. When you're moving along toward something desired, there are endless ways to slip off the path, more types of traps and distractions than there are fish in the sea. When things you don't really want to give life to start tugging at you, and your body is pulled in a direction you weren't trying to go, the king's focus helps you get good at returning. No matter where you find yourself, you know the way back. You don't beat yourself up—that's a distraction, too, frankly—you just come back. When you've practiced this coming back in the microcosm of something like meditation, reading, prayer, or sudoku, the psychic muscle memory kicks in with less effort when you need it for the big stuff.

And when you loathe something, when you find your thoughts in a loop of disparaging or unhelpful patterns, you can also redirect. You can simply take your attention and place it somewhere else. Whether a thought is echoing the energy of a relationship with the parent you struggled the most with, bringing up misery, or trying to keep you small and suffering, you have the power to take your attention elsewhere. And when you do, the strength of that thought diminishes. What was once a powerful activating force becomes weaker. This is how the king wields the power over life and death. It is very simple, and also quite hard. But like most things, with practice it gets easier.

Catherine MacCoun has written that "control of attention is thus the first skill an aspiring magician must master, and perhaps the most important." *Control* is a tricky word when it comes to internal events—I personally don't believe we *can* control things like thoughts or feelings, for instance. But I do think that, to an extent, and it will vary depending on the way our brains and environments are, we can hone our ability to put focus on what we wish to give value, what we wish to worship. As far as whether this is the first thing we need to learn, I'd suggest we go where our natural abilities lie in order to build strength and competence in things that come more easily to us before we toil in the realms that are more challenging. But I'll leave this for you, aspiring magician, to determine for yourself.

SECTION III

Tarot Reading

t was with some hesitation that I included a section about how to read cards in this book. I've always felt that tarot is an intuitive practice first and foremost, best learned creatively, instinctually, and taking into account the particulars of your own circumstances. When I got my first deck, I spent about two years pulling one card every morning and evening. Through that slow process of getting to know the cards, I also got to know myself. That was exactly what I needed from the cards when we first got together. Still, there are things I've learned over the years that I (and my editor) thought you might like to know.

The first thing I want to say before I share anything that resembles a how-to or that might be taken as a protocol is this: Nothing I will say here is to be taken as hard and fast. You will need to get out your sword and decide for yourself what's of use and what isn't, what may be valuable now, and what might need to be tucked away until later. I still go back to my first tarot book (Rachel Pollack's *Seventy-Eight Degrees of Wisdom*) and find secrets that are everything now but meant nothing back then. Give yourself the freedom and flexibility to do this.

The second thing I want to say is that tarot reading is an art, not a technical practice. This isn't to say art doesn't require technique, it does. And it isn't to say there's something better about one or the other; they each have their strengths. A technician is a beautiful thing to be, but it's not what we're doing here. We're not monitoring levels or keeping spreadsheets, though you can certainly do that if it helps you learn. In fact, when I was first getting to know the cards, my friend

Janice Fitch—who was much further along in her tarot journey than I was at the time—taught me to keep a notebook with a page for each card where I'd log notes and interpretations that I found useful. That notebook later formed the basis of how I understood each of the cards, and to this day I still pull it out sometimes when I do readings.

So use spreadsheets and logs if it's helpful, just don't let it restrict the less orderly aspects of the work: attending to energy; reawakening the part of you that can see into the subterranean; assuming a soft, wide gaze rather than a hard, focused one; catching dreams. This is a practice of collecting secrets and of keeping them—not in a clinging sense of the word but a preservative one—so you'll need to also develop a capacity for patience, reverence for the invisible, and trustworthiness.

A tarot practice can help you learn to do a very particular kind of balancing act between what you can know and what you can't, organization and incoherence, the village and the forest, the Emperor and Empress. So I'm going to give a bit of structure here to get you going— some charms for the road—but don't get boxed in. Tarot will remind you both that you are not alone and that your particular path is yours and you alone can walk it.

Tuck this into your back pocket before you go: The ideal of the World is plurality. It is neither to adopt a perfect protocol nor to reject the rules altogether, to identify as solely individual or collective, but to activate your capacity for a kind of kaleidoscopic awareness where you're able to hold many truths at once, to move fluidly and flexibly as each moment calls for.

Choosing a Deck

eople often ask which deck is best for beginners, and my answer is almost always the same: it's really up to you. It has to be. Part of what we're doing with tarot is learning to engage with the material world in a different way than what we're used to, learning to treat what we've been taught to perceive as an *inanimate* object—cards, in this case—as having an energy and life force all its own. Of being something worthy of respect, and of being deeply listened to. As Aleister Crowley wrote, "The cards of the Tarot are living individuals."

If we can manage this subtle shift in relationship when we work with cards, we wind up doing a lot more than just learning to read tarot. We start to move from a unilateral subject-object way of relating and toward one that hears, responds, and collaborates. We start edging into the World territory, into a space characterized not by homogeneity but by connectedness and relationship between diverse textures, energies, and landscapes.

The deck that's best for you as a beginner is the one you feel most comfortable and inclined to spend time with. The one that speaks a familiar language, one that feels like home, even if you're still figuring out what home is. Familiarity doesn't require fluency, but that will probably come, too, the more time you spend. Choose a deck that you genuinely want to spend time with. One that inspires humility, curiosity, a real wanting to understand.

Once you find the right deck (and you may go through some before that happens, that's okay), you'll be living together for years to come, so you should choose accordingly. Don't choose a deck that you feel an urge to rush past when you see them in the common area. You want cards that more closely resemble the roommate you mostly like to check in with, trading tales from the day, or just sipping tea and sighing quietly.

You might notice that your interpersonal relationship tendencies spill over into your connection with the cards. Are you the type of person who has an inclination to force things, ignore your gut, do more than your share even when it doesn't feel good? Do you believe that you *should* feel a certain way about something when you actually don't and stay too long in the wrong situation out of obligation? Are you someone who often gets super excited in the early stages of a relationship and then loses interest? Do you want too much too soon and then get frustrated when things take time to develop? Do you allow yourself to walk away when it's time?

I've heard some truly intricate tales of drawn-out relationships with tarot decks—*well, the illustrator is a dear friend or a person whose work in another field I respect; a loved one gifted me this set on their deathbed; the artist is from where I'm from*, on and on and on—to explain why, despite having no real connection of their own with the cards, a person feels obligated to work with them. Watch out for that.

A therapist I used to see would always tell me that a romantic partner should feel—for both parties—like a book neither of you wants to put down. That doesn't mean you don't live your own lives, just that you're eager to get back, and definitely not dreading it. Choose a deck like that. One you're eager to come home to. One that calls out and speaks to you in a voice you can really hear. This might be one of those things in life we can't ever be 100 percent sure about, but to the best of your ability you can aim for a deck that's long-term-relationship material. Because the task of a new reader is to earn trust over time, and eventually to begin to hear and keep secrets.

Asking Questions

Many traditional styles of tarot reading begin with a question. The style of tarot that I practice and teach positions cards as tools not only for giving answers, but also for formulating new questions that may broaden your viewpoint and—to use a term from narrative therapy—*thicken* the story you came with. And when it comes to which questions to ask, determining this is an art in itself. It takes practice to learn to ask the kinds of questions that, in the words of Clarissa Pinkola Estés, "cause the secret doors of the psyche to swing open."

When I give readings, I encourage people to use open-ended questions, or even frame queries in the form of intentions if that feels good, when consulting the cards. For instance, someone could ask, "What do I need to be aware of right now?" "What am I not seeing?" or "What secrets do you have to tell me today?"

If you're pulling cards for yourself, those are good starting points, but you might also choose to phrase your query in the form of an intention, like this: "I'm aiming for deeper clarity around this issue," or "I wish to broaden my perspective and see what is on the periphery, not the center," or "I am listening for what secrets the cards wish to tell me about how to be more loving/compassionate/gentle/authoritative/empowered" or whatever else you're going for.

I avoid yes or no questions as a practical way to make space for liminality—what lies between—because life is not so cut-and-dried.

You can certainly use the cards to tell you what to do but asking yes or no questions may narrow the possibilities for edging into unanticipated spaces, to do new learning. I prefer to work with cards as if we—my cards and I—are collaborators; we each give something, receive something, and stay willing to do our part.

Shuffling

As I'm thinking about the query—whether my own or that of the person I'm working with—I shuffle. I shuffle using the overhand style, which is when you hold the deck in one hand and use the other to draw small chunks out and then integrate them back into the deck so that they're dispersed differently than they were before. Depending on the size of the cards, I'll occasionally use the riffle style of shuffling, which is when you divide the cards into two piles and hold one in each hand, and then fold the two piles into one another. In this method, the top edges of the cards should overlap, so that the two piles are woven together in a new order.

As a rule, new cards are awkward to deal with. You simply need to spend time to build trust. Both of you will loosen up as you get to know each other, but new cards really repel smoothness—and that goes for shuffling, interpreting, and reading—until they know they are safe with you. Some of my most cherished decks have been known to shoot themselves all over the place, going stiffer than boards of hickory the moment I so much as think about a shuffle. Consider this a natural and healthy stage of the relationship. It took me a couple of years with my current deck, a vintage Rider-Waite-Smith with matte finish, to get to a place of ease with shuffling. To this day, when I shuffle in front of a group—like in a class, for instance—we both tighten up; cards go flying. I've made the decision to let that be okay.

And how will you know when you've shuffled enough? I'd say it depends. If I'm pulling for myself, I'm done when I feel settled. I sometimes think of shuffling as a sort of grounding technique that can bring me back into the body, where I can access the parts of my imagination that light up best when I feel rooted. To get here, I might focus on the temperature and texture of the cards, or the quality of my breath.

If I'm pulling for someone else, I'm shuffling while listening, so I might shuffle until I have a clear sense of, not the *question* per se, but the energy of what's needed. This is subtle, takes practice, and requires a kind of listening into liminality—between the lines of what's being explicitly stated—that we're not all used to. I'm listening for things like, Is this person's spirit anticipatory in a good way, or in a difficult-to-work-with way? Is their heart frightened, or lonely? Do they need to be supported or frustrated? Once I have a sense of that, I can stop shuffling.

If you're in the early days of your practice and this all feels like too tall an order, rein it in and keep it simple: Shuffle until the cards are in a different enough order than they were when you picked them up. Imagine that your energy is intermingling with them, and theirs with you. If you feel fearful or anxious, notice that and know it is okay to feel that way. No need to get rid of any feeling that's coming up, but see if you can temper it with some curiosity.

Once I'm done shuffling the cards, I—and you're welcome to use this method, but the best thing to do is find a way that feels good for you—divide them into three piles, facedown, in a horizontal row. Then I take the middle pile, put it on top of the left side pile, and then put that stack on top of the right-side pile. I draw each card from the top, placing the cards facedown on the table as I pull them.

When it's time to turn them over, I turn them all over at once. I like to see the full picture and find that, for me personally, secrets are more audible that way. But you may find that turning them one at a time is the best way to activate and amplify what wants to emerge. Take the time to experiment and listen for what's best for you and the cards.

Spreads

preads are another opportunity to consider relationship dynamics. Have you ever met someone whom you clicked with right away, but then you went too deep, too fast? Looked up and realized you were way out in the middle of a huge body of water and so far from the shore you weren't sure you had the strength to swim back? Going deep safely requires a foundation of trust and understanding. And though it might be tempting when the chemistry is there to go really far and deep, you want to be sure there's a foundation of trust that can sustain it.

People often come to tarot with preconceptions about what the cards can and can't do. For instance, you might come to tarot with the idea that the cards are going to tell you your life and future, that they have the power to control your destiny or summon things to happen and so forth. I am not here to tell you what the cards can and can't do, and a lot of that is going to depend on how you use them and what your particular gifts are. But as you figure those things out, which will take time, take it easy. Spend time building an understanding of what you and the cards are capable of, together. Don't go in deeper than the trust between you can support. Think about it this way: If you wouldn't expect a new friend or lover to tell you all their secrets in the first month of getting to know each other, maybe approach your cards with a similar respect. Elaborate ten-card spreads might be too much when you're just getting to know each other.

As I mentioned earlier, when I got my first deck, I spent about two years pulling one card every morning and evening. I was doing a lot of personal healing work at that time, learning how to regulate emotions, trust myself, and cope with grief in ways that didn't beget more pain in the long run. I'd generally ask something along the lines of "What do I need to know regarding x, y, or z?" and then look up the meaning for the card I'd drawn using books and write-ups on the internet. I logged ideas in a blank notebook with a page for each of the seventy-eight cards until I had a complete book full of my favorite interpretations. Later, I used that book to give my first readings, until one day a friend encouraged me to put it away. "You know these cards in and out," he said. It took putting the book away for me to realize that, to an extent, he was right. Of course, years later, I'm still having revelations, maybe even more than ever. The beautiful thing is, because the cards shape-shift in context, I don't think the revelations ever stop.

Some people interpret cards differently depending on whether the card is upright or reversed in a spread. I've never read reversals, and this is a personal choice. To me, any "reversed" meaning has always felt inherent in the upright; for instance if an artist is feeling blocked creatively and they draw the Empress upright, it's obvious that the Empress is not saying, "Oh yes, your creative juices are flowing," but rather she's asking questions about what needs to happen in order to get a generative energy moving again. If a person's emotions are making it difficult to see the facts of a matter, an upright Queen of Swords may show up as an invitation, an ideal, or a guide. She need not be in reverse for the querent to get the idea and glean the medicine. Through my years of practice, it's generally been clear when a quality, energy, or skill shows up in the cards that's missing or needs to be cultivated in the querent.

To those who work with reversals, mine is likely an oversimplified view of what they can mean or how they can be used. If you're interested in working with the cards in this way and aren't currently, I'd suggest exploring them in your practice and seeking guidance from readers you trust who have developed a good working relationship with inverted cards.

After a couple of years pulling one card in the morning and one in the evening, I started to experiment with combinations. I'd pull three cards instead of just one and listen for how they interacted with one another. You definitely don't *need* to spend two years pulling only one card at a time, but you should do what feels manageable for you and what allows you to really get to know them both as individuals and as part of a whole. If pulling a ten-card spread on the day you get your cards feels like the right thing for you, go for it! At the end of the day, this is always going to be a practice of listening closely for what works. You're going to keep coming back to that lesson.

Three-card spreads are an excellent stepping-stone from one-card draws to larger, more complex spreads. Many people like to assign "past, present, future" values to a three-card spread. I, personally, shy away from chronological approaches to interpreting spreads. I really can't speak to using cards to divine the future; that's just not what I do. But if you want to try a "past, present, future" spread, you might do so by asking something like, "What do I need to be aware of?" for each position in time. This way, you're not necessarily predicting what will happen, but laying down a doorway to walk through—a threshold to cross over—where you might gain access to a new detail that you may not have otherwise noticed.

I feel it's important for me to say again that what I'm about to share is by no means the one way to do things. I'm sharing it simply in hopes that it might be helpful for you to hear what I do. And my highest ideal is to be supportive of your finding a way that truly works for you. You are, of course, welcome to adopt this way as your own if that feels right. You are equally invited to take what bits and pieces work and toss the rest.

When I do a three-card pull, I draw the cards from my shuffled pile and place them facedown in a horizontal row. Unlike some of the more classic spreads (such as the Celtic Cross or even "past, present, future" three-card draws), I don't give the positions assigned meanings (such as obstacle or outcome), and I don't view them in any chronological order. Rather, I think about each card as if it were a doorway to walk through and poke around in, see what's there. Sometimes it'll feel like tumbling through the back of a magical wardrobe, others will look more like a broom closet. Maybe there's a charm somewhere in there, but it's hiding in the corner covered with generations of dust and you'll only get a glimpse if you really look hard.

And speaking of looking, there's an art to it when you're working with cards. "Looking hard" isn't quite what you're going for, really; what you want to be doing is looking broad, looking wide, opening your gaze to incorporate what's on the edges. Let me give a couple of examples to help articulate what I mean. It's a bit tricky, by design.

While I was writing this book I started learning to ride a horse. My teacher taught me to keep my eyes in the direction I wanted to go, but she noticed that I was spending most of my time looking at the horse's ears. It was sweet, she said. But really, it was a kind of hypervigilance. I didn't trust the horse, myself, or the process, so I watched diligently, waiting for him to throw his head back, buck his hind legs, or burst into a gallop before I was ready. As if my watching his ears like some sort of red-tailed predator was going to do anything for me in the event something like that did happen.

That kind of hard looking, where the gaze is zoned in on one very specific point, is good in some cases. Like when you're trying to solve certain kinds of problems, or when you're doing something really precise. On horseback, though, and in a lot of other contexts, it's a liability. Laser focus negates your ability to notice when the farm dog comes flying out of nowhere, or when there's a tree down up ahead and the trail's too narrow to turn around. So the task when you're riding is to broaden your vision to incorporate and become part of the whole. It's an old way of seeing, and that's the kind of seeing we want to do with tarot.

Keepers of old secrets—whether storytellers, tarot readers, cowboys, or elders—will tell you that the solutions in a crisis always emerge from the edges, not the center. It's never the king who saves the day. Or the knight with all the privilege and grooming. It's the absolute fool who comes riding in on a donkey with the ill-fitting armor, the poor man who fibbed his way into the royal party, the youngest daughter that no one would dare put their ducats on. Once I understood this, I started to see it everywhere. If you practice softening your gaze when you look at things, I think you'll start seeing it, too.

What does this have to do with tarot? The notion that what's needed is going to come from the margins hints at the importance of being able to open up around both the images in the cards and the particulars of our lives, to see them as also broad and wide rather than only sharp and narrow. At the center, much is certain, a lot is fixed. On the edges, though, you can see territories beyond your own. There's potential for cross-pollination, the sharing of ideas and resources. It's out there that you can start to see the center—the stuff you think you know for sure—in a new way. I can think of very few people who don't come to tarot, at least in the beginning, for a new way to see things.

So when you're pulling cards, you'll have ideas about what the cards mean, interpretations you love, associations you'll be eager to amplify. And you'll get to all that. But first, just notice. What are you feeling in your body? What memories are lighting up? What's your heart doing? Which feathers are getting ruffled? Where does the hair stand up? If you think you know what a card means right away, well, think again. As my old friend and artist Robert Tannen used to say, "Think that you might be wrong."

In certain schools of dreamwork it's often said that a dream will never tell you something you already know. I'm not sure I believe that—at least not in a literal sense—but it's not a bad way to open up to what might be on the edges. The obvious is like a siren's call, tempting. See if you can resist it. When the cards don't make immediate sense, see if you can be with that. What's the texture of the feeling when nothing resonates? What about certain symbols strikes you as neutral, uninteresting, or void of meaning? What about them bores you, shuts you down, or even gives rise to resistance?

In my earlier days of teaching about tarot, I used to always tell people that if you pull cards and they don't resonate, you're allowed to put them back and shuffle again. That's true. These days I'm a bit less hurried, more interested in a good thing that takes time to bloom. Mythologist Martin Shaw has said of old stories that if a story makes immediate logical sense, "it's not really doing its work," and I think the same can be said for tarot. You can always put the cards back and draw again, but do make room for the ones that like some time to aerate. Lay them out in a place that you'll see them and see if they shape-shift throughout the week. Make a habit of getting receptive to what wants to be seen rather than expecting revelations on demand. That just isn't how secrets work.

And since you've stuck with me all this time by now, I'll tell you a secret of my own: it is very rare that I draw cards and they make sense right away. Storyteller Martín Prechtel's advice for working with old stories by "feeding" them applies here: feed the cards with offerings. Some of the things my cards respond well to are curiosity, attention, and time. To build an energy of reciprocity, I like to ask the cards, "What questions do you have, for me?"

As more of us come around to the knowing that tarot can be used as a tool to take care of ourselves, I think it's really important to remember that self-care isn't always about feeling good. Our sense of entitlement to experiencing only nice feelings can often manifest, ultimately, as the antithesis of care. Is it truly self-care if it doesn't extend to all aspects of our experience, including—and perhaps especially—the things we'd rather reject, disown, or avoid altogether?

After all, the assumption that what feels good is good and what feels bad is to be avoided is incompatible with the philosophical underpinnings of tarot, which strive toward the totality of experience. The promise of the World's medicine is that it would impart in us an understanding that all aspects of our being have a role to play in our development. A regular practice of pulling cards is one of many ways available to develop this understanding on a visceral level, and to learn to live it. Each time we pull a card and remain open to what it might activate in us, we are carving out a safe, stable container in which we can learn to *be* with the stuff we'd rather not be with. And that can be life altering.

Conclusion

hen I was a kid, my mother—who is also a social worker and storyteller—had a set of Rider-Waite-Smith tarot cards, and I remember how strange they seemed. When I got my own cards many years later, I was inexplicably drawn back to that strangeness, like I was being summoned into a weird world unlike the one I'd grown accustomed to, one that was rational, logical, and a bit dry, if I'm honest.

Most of the books I'd read about the human experience up until that time had a sterility about them that felt stripped of what might be nutritive for some invisible, mysterious domain of my experience. And while I am indebted to those books for many things—emotional, behavioral, cognitive—there was a part of me they could never quite touch. That part was unable to absorb the cold metallic language of the manuals and self-help workbooks I'd been immersed in at my day job in psychology publishing.

Tarot did something different. Its visual metaphors sent ripples into an undercurrent that I'd always sensed was there but didn't know how to access. And as that layer of my being began to stir, I found myself drawn into a wider ebb and flow of something mythic. Something that locked me into a knowing that life—mine, the lives of the people around me, the inhabitants of earth and the cosmos at large—was ripe with hidden meaning. I think that's what religious experience is—nonrational experiences of something sacred.

Theologian Rudolf Otto developed the concept of the numinous, which professor of religion Stuart Sarbacker has described as "the experience of a mysterious terror and awe and majesty in the presence of that which is entirely other and thus incapable of being expressed directly through human language and other media." It was something that, to be understood, had to be experienced directly. I don't know how to talk about what that is, exactly. Truthfully, defining it is not an endeavor I have much interest in. But if we could learn to understand change—not intellectually but in a felt way as a law of life—keeping one foot on the ground and one in the mysteries, I think we'd be doing pretty well. And I think tarot is just one of many ways we can start to do that. Which is why I wanted to call this book *Tarot for Change.*

Many of the secrets shared in my reflections on the seventy-eight arcana incorporate ideas from therapies specifically designed to support people in making real change in their lives, through building awareness about the complex interaction of different domains of the human experience—the energetic, emotional, behavioral, and intellectual. But this is also a book about orienting ourselves toward the state of things, which is flux, the "natural ambiguity of life." It is a book of charms that I hope might help you not only cope with and learn from this inescapable natural reality, but even to embrace it, on a good day. And it's a book of old wisdom that must itself change in a modern context to meet the times, even as the core of these ideas remains faithful to the ancients. We've tracked the ways that ideas from as far back as ancient Egypt and Greece have cropped up in contemporary evidence-based psychotherapies and are being tapped today for their healing magic, though it likely won't be called that at a behavioral psychology conference anytime soon.

There are so many ways to boil down what's most beautiful about tarot. I could say one hundred different things, easily. I'll share just one here. If you choose to develop your own practice with these strange little cards, you'll get to know yourself better. You'll better understand what it means to be born into a human body, with the capacities to experience energy, feel, act, and think. But something else will also happen, and it's a really important something else.

Tarot will help you recall your self in a broader human context. It will do so in a way that reading a self-help book or even filling out pages in a workbook might not be able to do for you. Every card you pull will be like glimpsing a carving on an old rock or tree that reads, "[Someone] was here," the subtext being, you are not alone in your suffering, and your troubles are not new. These things have been experienced, understood, transmuted, and even philosophized about since time immemorial. Illness, heartbreak, deprivation, isolation, death, tragedy. Tales as old as time. Remembering this is a medicine.

Tarot for Change is an offering that came from years of a committed relationship with the cards themselves, and it is what became possible through that work, among other things: a heightened capacity for being in uncertainty, an understanding that doing my best and needing to do better are not mutually exclusive, and a willingness to display not only the parts of myself that I'm most proud of but also the holes in my thinking, the places where my understanding lacks discernment or grace or wisdom, the vulnerabilities.

And I hope that the reflections shared here—taken with the understanding that they've derived directly from my personal journey with tarot and life and the secrets the cards have told me—will support you in your own journey of finding what's possible, what you're here to do, and how to hold it all lightly, knowing it won't stay.

About the Author

Jessica Dore is a licensed social worker, tarot reader, writer and teacher. Dore has studied and worked in the fields of psychology and behavioural science publishing since 2010 and holds a master's degree in social work. She spent six years at self-help and psychology book publisher New Harbinger Publications and two years as book reviews editor at Psych Central. Her writing has appeared in O, *The Oprah Magazine*, *VICE* and Psych Central, and her unique approach to working with and interpreting tarot has been featured in *The New York Times*, *The Cut*, *Vogue*, *Yoga Journal* and many more publications. www.jessicadore.com

HAY HOUSE

Look within

Join the conversation about latest products, events, exclusive offers and more.

 f Hay House

 @HayHouseUK

 @hayhouseuk

We'd love to hear from you!